Contents

Introduction

The 2014 National Curriculum for Key Stages 1 and 2 explains the purpose and aims of history as follows:

A high-quality history education will help pupils gain a coherent knowledge and understanding of Britain's past and that of the wider world. It should inspire pupils' curiosity to know more about the past. Teaching should equip pupils to ask perceptive questions, think critically, weigh evidence, sift arguments, and develop perspective and judgement. History helps pupils to understand the complexity of people's lives, the process of change, the diversity of societies and relationships between different groups, as well as their own identity and the challenges of their time.

The National Curriculum for History aims to ensure that all children:
- *know and understand the history of these islands as a coherent, chronological narrative, from the earliest times to the present day: how people's lives have shaped this nation and how Britain has influenced and been influenced by the wider world*
- *know and understand significant aspects of the history of the wider world: the nature of ancient civilisations; the expansion and dissolution of empires; characteristic features of past non-European societies; achievements and follies of mankind*
- *gain and deploy a historically grounded understanding of abstract terms such as 'empire', 'civilisation', 'parliament' and 'peasantry'*
- *understand historical concepts such as continuity and change, cause and consequence, similarity, difference and significance, and use them to make connections, draw contrasts, analyse trends, frame historically valid questions and create their own structured accounts, including written narratives and analyses*
- *understand the methods of historical enquiry, including how evidence is used rigorously to make historical claims, and discern how and why contrasting arguments and interpretations of the past have been constructed*
- *gain historical perspective by placing their growing knowledge into different contexts, understanding the connections between local, regional, national and international history; between cultural, economic, military, political, religious and social history; and between short- and long-term timescales.*

The curriculum goes on to state that *children are expected to know, apply and understand the matters, skills and processes specified in the relevant programme of study*. There are two programmes of study in the primary history curriculum: one for Key Stage 1 and one for Key Stage 2. On its own, the content of the programmes of study is insufficient to create exciting and effective learning experiences. This series of books is designed to help provide guidance and support for schools, phase and subject leaders, coordinators and teachers, through a coherent, challenging, engaging and enjoyable scheme of work.

In this series, there is one book for Years 1 and 2, one for Years 3 and 4 and one for Years 5 and 6. The books contain planning for each year group, divided into six chapters, each covering half a term's worth of work. You can use the chapters within each book flexibly to suit the learning needs of the children in your class.

Each chapter is divided into six weeks, with most weeks containing two lessons. This timeframe is just a suggestion, and there is no need to stick to it – many of the chapters have broad cross-curricular links, and could be blocked into a shorter, more focused, 'topic' approach.

■ SCHOLASTIC

Terminology

In this guide, the main terms used are:

- **Lesson outcomes:** the skills and knowledge children should be able to demonstrate at the end of the lesson.
- **Curriculum objectives:** these are statutory requirements, taken directly from the National Curriculum for history, under the heading 'Children should be taught about'. Text in brackets is a simple summary of the main topic covered in that lesson.
- **Historical concepts:** these are the skills and knowledge children need to develop in order to become effective historians. They are taken directly from the first part of the subject content for the relevant key stage (before the heading 'Pupils should be taught about').

The new curriculum for history covers periods of history and areas of study that may be unfamiliar to many primary teachers. The 'Background knowledge' sections, at the end of the planning grid for each year group, support the understanding of unfamiliar terms, and provide background information on each topic of study.

Assessment

Assessment opportunities are given for each lesson. At the end of each chapter, there is an assessment lesson based on open-ended tasks that reinforce the learning, which provides teachers with guidance on what to look for and what questions to ask.

About the book

The book provides content for each year group (Years 1–6) and includes:

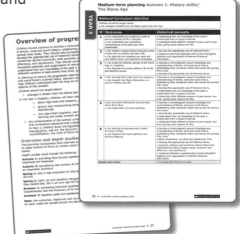

- **Long-term planning:** an overview of the areas of study, outcomes, curriculum objectives, focus questions and historical concepts covered in each half-termly chapter.
- **Medium-term planning:** six half-termly grids are provided for each year group. Each contains an overview of each week's planning, including the theme being covered, the outcomes for that week, and the attainment targets covered.
- **Progression:** year-by-year progression in historical concepts is outlined after each medium-term planning grid.
- **Background knowledge:** this explains key concepts, relevant to the year group, to help support teachers' knowledge.

About the CD-ROM

The CD-ROM provides the long-term planning, progression, medium-term planning and background knowledge as editable Word files. These can all be adapted to meet the needs of your school. From the menu screen on the CD-ROM, simply navigate to the year group you require and then click on the button to open the associated file.

About the poster

The poster summarises the progression of key concepts in the National Curriculum for history. Display it in a central location, such as the staffroom, to help improve understanding of the new curriculum within your school.

Year 1 Long-term planning

1. *Children should know and understand the history of these islands as a coherent, chronological narrative, from the earliest times to the present day: how people's lives have shaped this nation and how Britain has influenced and been influenced by the wider world.*

   Children study events, changes and people within living memory and beyond living memory and are able to place them in coherent timelines and in recounts.

2. *Children should know and understand significant aspects of the history of the wider world: the nature of ancient civilisations; the expansion and dissolution of empires; characteristic features of past non-European societies; achievements and follies of mankind.*

   Children will learn about the achievements of the Wright Brothers and their first aeroplane flight in the USA, as well as Bruegel the Elder and his paintings.

3. *Children should gain and deploy a historically grounded understanding of abstract terms such as 'empire', 'civilisation', 'parliament' and 'peasantry'.*

   Children are introduced to the terms 'monarchy', 'peasantry', 'United Kingdom' and 'heritage'.

4. *Children should understand historical concepts such as continuity and change, cause and consequence, similarity, difference and significance, and use them to make connections, draw contrasts, analyse trends, frame historically valid questions and create their own structured accounts, including written narratives and analyses.*

   Children are given the opportunity to learn about the above historical concepts, make connections and contrasts, ask and answer questions and write simple accounts and narratives.

5. *Children should understand the methods of historical enquiry, including how evidence is used rigorously to make historical claims, and discern how and why contrasting arguments and interpretations of the past have been constructed.*

   Children are introduced to historical enquiry and interpretations of the past through topics on shops, the Great Fire of London, Bruegel the Elder and LS Lowry, the first aeroplane flight, Victorian children at play and the heritage of the United Kingdom with a focus on folk tales and castles.

6. *Children should gain historical perspective by placing their growing knowledge into different contexts, understanding the connections between local, regional, national and international history; between cultural, economic, military, political, religious and social history; and between short- and long-term timescales.*

   Children are given opportunities to make links between their national and local history; carry out local studies; and use a range of empathetic activities such as role play, imaginative play and a range of sources to gain the beginnings of a historical perspective.

Overview and depth studies

The medium-term planning incorporates both overview topics and depth studies, but you may choose to adapt lessons in order to focus on certain topics in more detail, or to skip lessons in order to shorten topics. Depth studies could include the following:

Autumn 1: studying the way shops looked externally or internally, or items shops sold in the past; a local focus on shops

Autumn 2: the main fire events of the Great Fire of London; fire-fighting techniques; buildings during the Great Fire; diaries and oral accounts of the events

Spring 1: focus on one of the artists (Bruegel the Elder or LS Lowry); a comparison of a pair of paintings

Spring 2: the immediate events leading up to and including the 1903 first flight; the Wright Brothers' biography

Summer 1: Victorian toys and games; Victorian parks and pleasure gardens/local focus

Summer 2: castles, with or without a local focus; folk stories from around the United Kingdom

Note: the outcomes, objectives and concepts outlined in the medium-term planning grids are spread across two lessons

Overview of progression in Year 1

From the Foundation Stage, children should continue to develop an understanding of past and present events in their own lives and in the lives of family members. Throughout Year 1, they should be able to use common words and phrases relating to people, places, traditions and events and develop an increasing awareness of recent and distant past.

They also place pictures, objects or events in sequence. By the end of year, they are aware of where some historical periods fit beside each other.

Children should be able to recognise simple similarities and differences in relation to people, places, traditions and objects. Throughout Year 1, children are able to identify similarities and differences between ways of life in recent and distant history and start to make comparisons and contrasts. They also begin to become aware of the cause and effect of events or people's actions on how we see things.

Children should be able to ask and answer simple questions about events and stories from the past. Throughout Year 1, they collect and use a wider vocabulary of everyday historical words that enable them to ask and answer questions in more detail; they start to discuss their findings and thoughts. They use parts of stories and are introduced to a range of primary and secondary sources to show that they know and understand key features of events.

At the start of Year 1, children begin to understand some of the ways in which we find out about the past, by being shown a range of sources and guided on how to use them. They also develop enquiring skills as history detectives. By the end of Year 1, they begin to be more independent and aware of these ways of finding historical information.

At the beginning of Year 1, children listen to and discuss the different ways in which oral accounts can help them find out about recent history, changes and events. They should become more aware of other ways that history is represented and use it for discussion.

In planning to ensure the progression described above through teaching about the people, events and changes outlined below, teachers are often introducing children to historical periods that they will study more fully at Key Stages 2 and 3. In Year 1, these include the Anglo-Saxons, the medieval period, the Stuarts and the Victorians, the 20th century (in living memory and beyond) and links to various historical periods within the school's local area.

Throughout Year 1, children should be taught about:

- *changes within living memory. Where appropriate, these should be used to reveal aspects of change in national life*
  Children will learn how shops have changed since the 1930s and investigate LS Lowry's paintings to see how life has changed in industrial towns.

- *events beyond living memory that are significant nationally or globally*
  Children will learn about the Great Fire of London, the first aeroplane flight, lives of Victorian children, main events and people behind well-known folk stories of the United Kingdom.

- *the lives of significant individuals in the past who have contributed to national and international achievements. Some should be used to compare aspects of life in different periods*
  Children will learn about the lives and paintings of Bruegel the Elder and LS Lowry and compare the similarities and differences of life between Bruegel's 16th century Netherlands and LS Lowry's 20th century Lancashire. They will also learn about the achievements of the Wright Brothers, Sir Christopher Wren and the importance of Samuel Pepys's and John Evelyn's diary accounts of the Great Fire of London.

- *significant historical events, people and places in their own locality*
  There are opportunities in the chapters on shops, Victorian children at play (local parks) and our United Kingdom heritage (local castles and local folk stories) for the children to find out more about the history of their local area. The chapter on LS Lowry also allows children to use local buildings as part of their class mural. Schools near London or in industrial towns and cities could also arrange school trips to find out more about the Great Fire or the type of landscapes that inspired LS Lowry.

Medium-term planning Autumn 1: Shops since the 1930s

National Curriculum objective

Children should be taught about:
• changes within living memory. Where appropriate, these should be used to reveal aspects of change in national life

W	Outcomes	Historical concepts
1	• Know what shops are. • Can identify where they shop and what they buy. • Can sort photographs of shops into chronological order from the 1930s to the present.	• Develop an awareness of the past, using common words and phrases relating to the passing of time. • Know where people and events they study fit within a chronological framework. • Identify similarities and differences between ways of life in different periods. • Use a wide vocabulary of everyday historical terms. • Answer and ask questions, choosing stories and other sources to show that they know key features of events. • Understand ways in which we find out about the past.
2	• Can use sources to find out about the different types of shop and their names. • Can sort shops according to the type of goods they sold. • Know why some shops no longer exist. • Can create a diorama of an old shop front.	• (same as week 1)
3	• Can say how goods were ordered and then delivered to the door in the 1930s. • Can use historical vocabulary to create a simple delivery-list poem. • Can make connections with modern day home-delivery services. • Can investigate an old shop item from the past and its present day version. • Can draw and describes an object from the past and compare it with its present day products. • Know why some items are no longer around.	• Develop an awareness of the past, using common words and phrases relating to the passing of time. • Know where people and events they study fit within a chronological framework. • Identify similarities and differences between ways of life in different periods. • Use a wide vocabulary of everyday historical terms. • Answer and ask questions, choosing stories and other sources to show that they know and understand key features of events. • Understand some of the ways in which we find out about the past.
4	• Can use sources to find out about decorated biscuit and sweet tins from the past and sort them into design styles. • Can create a picture design for an old-fashioned sweet tin.	• Develop an awareness of the past, using common words and phrases relating to the passing of time. • Identify similarities and differences between ways of life in different periods. • Use a wide vocabulary of everyday historical terms. • Understand ways in which we find out about the past.
5	• Can use photographic sources to find out about the inside of a grocer's shop from the past. • Can use photographic evidence to create a class grocer's shop. • Use role play with the class 1930s shop to develop comparison, enquiry and empathy skills.	• Develop an awareness of the past, using common words and phrases relating to the passing of time. • Identify similarities and differences between ways of life in different periods. • Use a wide vocabulary of everyday historical terms. • Answer and ask questions. • Understand some of the ways in which we find out about the past.
6	• Understand what an oral account is and listen to oral accounts of shopping. • Create an oral questionnaire to use with family members. • Can use questionnaires to gather oral accounts about shops.	• Develop an awareness of the past, using common words and phrases relating to the passing of time. • Know where people and events they study fit within a chronological framework. • Use a wide vocabulary of everyday historical terms. • Identify similarities and differences between ways of life in different periods. • Answer and ask questions. • Understand some of the ways in which we find out about the past. • Identify different ways in which the past is represented.
Assess and review		• To assess the half-term's work.

Medium-term planning Autumn 2: The Great Fire of London

YEAR 1

National Curriculum objectives

Children should be taught about:
- events beyond living memory that are significant nationally or globally
- the lives of significant individuals in the past who have contributed to national and international achievements. Some should be used to compare aspects of life in different periods

W	Outcomes	Historical concepts
1	• Know when the Great Fire of London took place and understand what London was like in 1666. • Know who was king at the time of the Great Fire. • Can locate the date of Great Fire on a historical timeline of the United Kingdom. • Can understand how and where the Great Fire of London started. • Can understand why the Great Fire spread so quickly.	• Develop an awareness of the past, using common words and phrases relating to the passing of time. • Know where people and events they study fit within a chronological framework. • Identify similarities and differences between ways of life in different periods. • Use a wide vocabulary of everyday historical terms. • Ask and answer questions, choosing and using parts of stories and other sources to show that they know and understand key features of events. • Understand ways in which we find out about the past.
2	• Can label the features of a timber-framed house and tar paper shack. • Can understand why many buildings were destroyed in the Great Fire. • Can create 2D models using collage for a class frieze of London during the Great Fire.	• Identify similarities and differences between ways of life in different periods. • Use a wide vocabulary of everyday historical terms. • Ask and answer questions. • Understand some of the ways in which we find out about the past.
3	• Can use a range of sources to find out how the Great Fire was fought and make comparisons with present-day fire-fighting. • Can understand why poor fire-fighting methods failed to stop the Great Fire. • Are aware that 'London's Burning' is a song about the Great Fire of London. • Can write more verses of the rhyme using 17th century fire equipment and actions. • Can use rhymes to re-enact fighting the Great Fire.	• Develop an awareness of the past, using common words and phrases relating to the passing of time. • Identify similarities and differences between ways of life in different periods. • Use a wide vocabulary of everyday historical terms. • Ask and answer questions, choosing and using parts of stories and other sources to show that they know and understand key features of events. • Understand some of the ways in which we find out about the past. • Identify different ways in which the past is represented.
4	• Can use pictures and eyewitness accounts to find out how people fled and create a group diary of the Great Fire's events. • Can investigate pictures and eyewitness accounts to help them re-enact escaping the fire in a drama session.	• (same as week 3)
5	• Can place the events of the Great Fire of London in chronological order. • Can use oral accounts to find out where the homeless of the Great Fire lived. • Can compare these tent camps with present day disaster camps. • Can empathise with the Great Fire homeless and create posters to ask for aid.	• Develop an awareness of the past, using common words and phrases relating to the passing of time. • Know where people and events they study fit within a chronological framework. • Identify similarities and differences between ways of life in different periods. • Use a wide vocabulary of everyday historical terms. • Ask and answer questions. • Understand ways in which we find out about the past. • Identify different ways in which the past is represented.
6	• Know about the good and bad effects on London after the Great Fire. • Know about Sir Christopher Wren and can draw his portrait. • Can review their work on the topic. • Know about the Christopher Wren Monument and understand why it was built. • Can design a new top for the Monument.	• Develop an awareness of the past, using common words and phrases relating to the passing of time. • Know where people and events they study fit within a chronological framework. • Use a wide vocabulary of everyday historical terms. • Ask and answer questions. • Understand ways in which we find out about the past. • Identify different ways in which the past is represented.
Assess and review		• To assess the half-term's work.

Medium-term planning Spring 1: Bruegel the Elder and LS Lowry (investigating pictures)

National Curriculum objectives

Children should be taught about:
- the lives of significant individuals in the past who have contributed to national and international achievements. Some should be used to compare aspects of life in different periods
- changes within living memory. Where appropriate, these should be used to reveal aspects of change in national life
- significant historical events, people, places in their own locality

W	Outcomes	Historical concepts
1	• Can investigate self-portraits of Pieter Bruegel the Elder and LS Lowry to find out when they lived and who they were. • Know how people lived in the 16th century. • Can explain why Bruegel was called 'Peasant Bruegel'.	• (same as week 3)
2	• Can investigate the games shown in Bruegel's *Children's Games* and compare them to present day games. • Can recreate Bruegel's *Children's Games* with a large class photograph of modern children's games.	• Develop an awareness of the past, using common words and phrases relating to the passing of time. • Identify similarities and differences between ways of life in different periods. • Use a wide vocabulary of everyday historical terms. • Ask and answer questions. • Understand ways in which we find out about the past.
3	• Know when and where LS Lowry lived. • Can use pictures and oral accounts to find out about Lancashire cotton mills and the working conditions of the workers in the 1920s. • Can use historical language to identify features in a Lowry mill painting. • Can understand why LS Lowry painted mills and their workers.	• Develop an awareness of the past, using common words and phrases relating to the passing of time. • Know where people and events they study fit within a chronological framework. • Identify similarities and differences between ways of life in different periods. • Use a wide vocabulary of everyday historical terms. • Ask and answer questions. • Understand ways in which we find out about the past. • Identify different ways in which the past is represented.
4	• Can study the way buildings are created in Lowry's paintings and use photographs of local buildings to draw and paint Lowry-style buildings for the class mural. • Can label and draw in the missing features of buildings created in the style of LS Lowry. • Can draw a picture of their home in the style of LS Lowry.	• Identify similarities and differences between ways of life in different periods. • Use a wide vocabulary of everyday historical terms. • Ask and answer questions, choosing and using parts of stories and other sources to show that they know and understand key features of events. • Understand some of the ways in which we find out about the past.
5	• Know how LS Lowry figures are created. • Use finger painting techniques to paint Lowry-style figures or animals. • Know why Lowry's figures have been called matchstick people. • Can draw a matchstick character and write a short description about them.	• (same as week 2)
6	• Can give an account of a character in Bruegel's *The Peasant Wedding* and Lowry's *VE Day*. • Can write a thank you letter to the bride and bridegroom in a Bruegel painting. • Can identify similarities between two paintings. • Can understand how we can use the artists' work to find out about the past. • Can create paintings of their school for children in the future.	• (same as week 3)
Assess and review		• To assess the half-term's work.

■ SCHOLASTIC

Medium-term planning Spring 2: The first aeroplane flight

National Curriculum objectives

Children should be taught about:
- events beyond living memory that are significant nationally or globally
- changes within living memory. Where appropriate, these should be used to reveal aspects of change in national life
- the lives of significant individuals in the past who have contributed to national and international achievements. Some should be used to compare aspects of life in different periods

W	Outcomes	Historical concepts
1	• Can sort photographs and pictures of aeroplanes and put them in chronological order. • Know what flying machines from the past look like. • Know about people from long ago who wanted to invent flying machines. • Can draw one of the flying machines and label its features. • Can understand why some flying machines were not successful.	• Develop an awareness of the past, using common words and phrases relating to the passing of time. • Know where people and events they study fit within a chronological framework. • Identify similarities and differences between ways of life in different periods. • Use a wide vocabulary of everyday historical terms. • Ask and answer questions, choosing and using parts of stories and other sources to show that they know and understand key features of events. • Understand ways in which we find out about the past.
2	• Know who Orville and Wilbur Wright were and where and when they lived. • Know what made the brothers want to invent flying machines. • Can put instructions for a model toy helicopter into the right order. • Know that the Wright brothers became inventors and designed and built bicycles. • Can compare 'high wheel' bicycles and the 'Wright Brothers' safety bicycles.	• Develop an awareness of the past, using common words and phrases relating to the passing of time. • Know where people and events they study fit within a chronological framework. • Use a wide vocabulary of everyday historical terms. • Ask and answer questions, choosing and using parts of stories and other sources to show that they know and understand key features of events. • Understand some of the ways in which we find out about the past.
3	• Can understand how designing and making large kites helped the Wright brothers to design an aeroplane. • Can fly kites to investigate how they move in different directions.	• Use a wide vocabulary of everyday historical terms. • Know where people and events they study fit within a chronological framework. • Ask and answer questions, choosing and using parts of stories and other sources to show that they know and understand key features of events. • Understand some of the ways in which we find out about the past.
4	• Know what gliders are. • Can learn how they experimented with gliders at Kitty Hawk. • Can label a Wright glider. • Can make their own models to discover how the Wright brothers used gliders. • Can make their own Wright Brothers glider.	• (same as week 3)
5	• Know what happened on 17 December 1903. • Can put a recount of the day in the correct order. • Can write a poem about what it would be like to fly for the first time.	• (same as week 2)
6	• Can find out what the Wright Brothers did from 1903 to 1911. • Can think of questions that they would like to ask the brothers and use them in a hot-seat session. • Know that in 2003 it was the 100 year anniversary of the first aeroplane flight. • Can design a special stamp to commemorate the occasion.	• Develop an awareness of the past, using common words and phrases relating to the passing of time. • Know where people and events they study fit within a chronological framework. • Use a wide vocabulary of everyday historical terms. • Choose and use parts of stories and other sources to show that they understand key features of events. • Understand ways in which we find out about the past. • Identify different ways in which the past is represented.
Assess and review		• To assess the half-term's work.

Medium-term planning Summer 1: Victorian children at play

National Curriculum objectives

Children should be taught about:
- changes within living memory. Where appropriate, these should be used to reveal aspects of change in national life
- significant historical events, people, places in their own locality

W	Outcomes	Historical concepts
1	• Know who Queen Victoria was and that she lived a long time ago. • Can use sources to make a family tree of Queen Victoria's family. • Know about the difference between rich and poor children in Victorian times by looking at photographs and paintings.	• Develop an awareness of the past, using common words and phrases relating to the passing of time. • Know where people and events they study fit within a chronological framework. • Identify similarities and differences between ways of life in different periods. • Use a wide vocabulary of everyday historical terms. • Ask and answer questions, choosing and using parts of stories and other sources to show that they know and understand key features of events. • Understand ways in which we find out about the past. • Identify different ways in which the past is represented.
2	• Can learn how rich and poor Victorian children played, by trying out a range of their games and toys. • Can make simple Victorian toys.	• Develop an awareness of the past, using common words and phrases relating to the passing of time. • Identify similarities and differences between ways of life in different periods. • Use a wide vocabulary of everyday historical terms. • Understand ways in which we find out about the past.
3	• Know the sort of music poor Victorian children may have listened to, and how they heard them. • Can sing some popular Victorian songs. • Know the sort of music rich Victorian children may have listened to, and how they heard them.	• (same as week 1)
4	• Know why going to parks was so popular in Victorian times. • Can sort out photographs of parks from Victorian times to the present and put them in chronological order. • Can compare Victorian playground equipment with present-day equipment.	• Develop an awareness of the past, using common words and phrases relating to the passing of time. • Know where people and events they study fit within a chronological framework. • Identify similarities and differences between ways of life in different periods. • Use a wide vocabulary of everyday historical terms. • Ask and answer questions, choosing and using parts of stories and other sources to show that they know and understand key features of events. • Understand ways in which we find out about the past.
5	• Know about the features of a Victorian pleasure garden and can compare it with modern day pleasure gardens. • Can work together to create a class model of a Victorian pleasure garden.	• Develop an awareness of the past, using common words and phrases relating to the passing of time. • Identify similarities and differences between ways of life in different periods. • Use a wide vocabulary of everyday historical terms. • Ask and answer questions, choosing and using parts of stories and other sources to show that they know and understand key features of events. • Understand ways in which we find out about the past.
6	• Can understand that cheap train fares allowed less wealthy children to visit pleasure gardens for a treat. • Can draw a train poster to advertise a Victorian Pleasure gardens. • Can give an oral recount as a Victorian child and create a storyboard about a day trip to their local Victorian park.	• (same as week 1)
Assess and review		• To assess the half-term's work.

Medium-term planning Summer 2: Our United Kingdom heritage (folk stories and castles)

National Curriculum objectives

Children should be taught about:
- events beyond living memory that are significant nationally or globally
- significant historical events, people, places in their own locality

W	Outcomes	Historical concepts
1	• Can understand the term, 'United Kingdom' and can locate the four main regions on a map. • Can locate where they live. • Know the four historic symbols of the United Kingdom and can create ones for their local area.	• Develop an awareness of the past, using common words and phrases relating to the passing of time. • Use a wide vocabulary of everyday historical terms. • Ask and answer questions, choosing and using parts of stories and other sources to show they know and understand key feature of events.
2	• Can understand that the United Kingdom has many castles. • Know what castles were used for. • Can create a simple timeline of a local castle.	• Know where people and events they study fit within a chronological framework. • Identify similarities and differences between ways of life in different periods. • Ask and answer questions, choosing and using parts of stories and other sources to show that they know and understand key features of events.
3	• Know the features of a castle. • Can make a model of a castle.	• Identify similarities and differences between ways of life in different periods. • Use a wide vocabulary of everyday historical terms. • Understand some of the ways in which we find out about the past.
4	• Know about the different people who lived in a castle and their roles. • Can write a simple recount of an event or story that happened at their local castle.	• Develop an awareness of the past, using common words and phrases relating to the passing of time. • Know where people and events they study fit within a chronological framework. • Use a wide vocabulary of everyday historical terms. • Understand some of the ways in which we find out about the past.
5	• Can understand what folk tales are and how they are told worldwide. • Can understand the events, characters and messages in different folk tales. • Can work in groups to retell one of the folk tales orally.	• Use a wide vocabulary of everyday historical terms. • Ask and answer questions, choosing and using parts of stories and other sources to show that they know and understand key features of events. • Understand some of the ways in which we find out about the past. • Identify different ways in which the past is represented.
6	• Can use drama or storytelling to retell a local folk tale.	• Use a wide vocabulary of everyday historical terms. • Ask and answer questions, choosing and using parts of stories and other sources to show that they know and understand key features of events. • Understand some of the ways in which we find out about the past.
Assess and review		• To assess the half-term's work.

Year 1 Background knowledge

In Year 1, there is a varied range of topics that follow the main four curriculum objectives – changes within living memory, events beyond living memory, lives of significant individuals, and significant historical events, people and places in their locality. However, generic history skills should develop as the year progresses so these have been woven into the content planning. Some of these important history skills and themes are listed below:

Awareness of time and simple chronological frameworks

In Year 1, children should use simple common words and phrases that relate to the passing of time. Initially, these can be developed by describing events in their own lives or through recounting stories and then by describing changes in events in recent history. In the teacher book use of this vocabulary is encouraged for the first few lessons of each chapter. Children should learn about chronological sequence. This can be done by placing objects and pictures into a time sequence, such as photographs of shops or parks, or artefacts such as shop items. Events can also be put into a chronological order, through timelines, oral recounts, drama or written recounts and by retelling folk stories from around the United Kingdom.

Similarity and difference – a sense of the past

One of the earliest natural skills in history is a child's awareness of what is similar and what is different in past objects, pictures, stories and events compared to their own lives. In Year 1, children look deeper into these comparisons; they get the opportunity to listen to oral accounts, and study pictures and artefacts to investigate comparisons between present and past times, such as shops in 1930s and games played in the 1500s. Re-enactment, role play and imaginative play help reinforce these skills and develop empathy for what life was like in the past. Children are also able to make simple comparisons between different parts of society within one period of history, such as the lives of rich and poor Victorian children.

Cause and consequence

Children start to discuss the causes of events or reasons why people did things and the consequences they had for society. For example, in the chapter on Bruegel the Elder and LS Lowry, children find out why the artists decided to paint the lives of the working class and the importance of these pictures today. They discover how certain changes over time can have consequences, such as the decline of traditional shops due to supermarkets, as well as understanding how a combined set of causes of an event can have far-reaching consequences, such as the Great Fire of London, which resulted in a safer, cleaner city.

Asking and answering questions

Children progress from asking and answering simple questions about events or stories from the past, to using different sources of information to be able to make their own enquiries and deduce the answers. These can be encouraged by investigating 1930s shopping bags, studying a local artefact, festival or folk story, trying out medieval or Victorian games or experimenting with model gliders. Imaginative play allows children to develop their enquiry and empathy skills such as a class 1930s shop, a folk tale storytelling corner or a Wright brothers' inventors den. Other activities could include a controlled burning of a class model of London before the Great Fire, encouraging prediction and further questioning skills.

Constructing and interpreting the past from evidence

Children begin to talk about evidence and artefacts which give us information about the past. For example, in the chapter on shops, children use photographs, film and oral accounts to look at local or national changes in shops. Other evidence and artefacts used in the chapters include: paintings, newspaper accounts, stories, songs and music, day trips and a range of artefacts and multimedia. Children start to learn that the past can be interpreted in different ways by discovering that people have different points of view or experiences. For example, children listen to oral accounts of older people's memories, explore experiences of Londoners in the Great Fire and investigate how Lowry and Bruegel saw life in their times.

Reinforcement activities

Children are given opportunities to create artwork as a way to reinforce their knowledge or support skills in chronology, historical enquiry and deduction and in using and interpreting sources and artefacts. These include making a 2D mural of the city of London, decorating old-fashioned sweet tins, and making model castles, gliders and Victorian toys. Children also create modern-day versions of large friezes of Bruegel and LS Lowry paintings, a model of a Victorian pleasure gardens as well as re-enactments of national or local folk tales.

Year 2 Long-term planning

1. *Children should know and understand the history of these islands as a coherent, chronological narrative, from the earliest times to the present day: how people's lives have shaped this nation and how Britain has influenced and been influenced by the wider world.*
   Children learn about events, changes and people within living memory, such as the development of telephones, a local history focus and World War II. They also look at topics beyond living memory, such as the Gunpowder Plot, a local history focus, Elizabeth Fry's prison reform work and how Victorian Britain influenced the world through the Great Exhibition. In each chapter, timelines and comparisons help children put these areas into a chronological narrative.

2. *Children should know and understand significant aspects of the history of the wider world: the nature of ancient civilisations; the expansion and dissolution of empires; characteristic features of past non-European societies; achievements and follies of mankind.*
   Children learn about the stand against racial segregation by Rosa Parks in the US in the 1950s, and the role the Great Exhibition played in building the British Empire.

3. *Children should gain and deploy a historically grounded understanding of abstract terms such as 'empire', 'civilisation', 'parliament' and 'peasantry'.*
   Children are introduced to the terms, 'parliament', 'monarchy', 'segregation' and 'empire'.

4. *Children should understand historical concepts such as continuity and change, cause and consequence, similarity, difference and significance, and use them to make connections, draw contrasts, analyse trends, frame historically valid questions and create their own structured accounts, including written narratives and analyses.*
   Children are given the opportunity to learn about the above historical concepts, make connections, draw contrasts, ask and answer historically valid questions and write their simple accounts, narratives and explanations.

5. *Children should understand the methods of historical enquiry, including how evidence is used rigorously to make historical claims, and discern how and why contrasting arguments and interpretations of the past have been constructed.*
   Children deepen their skills in historical enquiry through all six topics – telephones, the Gunpowder Plot, Rosa Parks and Elizabeth Fry, the Great Exhibition, children in World War II, and our heritage.

6. *Children should gain historical perspective by placing their growing knowledge into different contexts, understanding the connections between local, regional, national and international history; between cultural, economic, military, political, religious and social history; and between short- and long-term timescales.*
   Children are given opportunities to make links between their national and local history; discuss the international effects of Rosa Parks' actions and the Great Exhibition; carry out a local study of a significant place, event or person; and use a range of empathetic activities, imaginative play and a range of sources to gain a historical perspective.

Overview and depth studies

The medium-term planning incorporates both overview topics and depth studies, but you may choose to adapt lessons to focus on certain topics in more detail or to skip lessons to shorten topics. Depth studies could include the following:

Autumn 1: comparisons of telephones over the ages; a study on Alexander Graham Bell

Autumn 2: the main event of the Gunpowder Plot; a depth study of the Shetlands' winter fire festival, Up Helly Aa

Spring 1: focus on Rosa Parks or Elizabeth Fry

Spring 2: building the Crystal Palace; visiting and exhibits

Summer 1: evacuation

Summer 2: class investigation into, or a class production about, a historical aspect of their local area

Note: the outcomes, objectives and concepts outlined in the medium-term planning grids for each week are spread across two lessons

Overview of progression in Year 2

Throughout Year 2, children should be more confident in using a wider range of common words and phrases relating to people, places, traditions and events and develop an increasing awareness of recent and distant past. They should also be able to place pictures, photographs, objects or events in sequence. By the end of Year 2, the children should have an understanding of how short- and long-term timescales fit beside each other, and the chronological order of recent and distant historical periods.

In Year 2, children continue to develop their skills in identifying similarities and differences between ways of life in recent and distant history and are expected to make more detailed comparisons and contrasts. They should also become more aware of the cause and effect of events or people's actions and how they have influenced the present.

In Key Stage 1, children should ask and answer questions, referring to stories and other sources. In Year 2, they should develop more confidence in their enquiring abilities by becoming history detectives and asking more pertinent questions about artefacts, why events happened, why people acted the way they did and how things were significant or made a difference to society locally, nationally or internationally. Throughout these Year 2 topics, children collect and use a wider vocabulary of everyday historical words that enable them to ask and answer questions in more detail and talk about features and concepts such as segregation with understanding.

Children should understand some of the ways in which we find out about the past. In Year 2, children listen to and interpret stories, as well as more primary and secondary sources, to gain a deeper understanding of the past. They should show an understanding of how these sources can help them to know and comprehend key features of events. In the last chapter in Year 2, which focuses on a local history project, all these skills should come together so that the children can effectively explore a significant event, person or place in their own locality.

At the end of Year 1, children began to explore how oral accounts of recent and distant events are an important source of information. In Year 2, children begin to discover that there can be different versions or viewpoints of the same event, which makes the event seem slightly different.

In planning to ensure the progression described above through teaching about the people, events and changes outlined below, children are introduced to historical periods that they will study more fully at Key Stages 2 and 3. In the Year 2 chapters these historical periods are: the early Stuarts (James I), the early 19th century, the Victorians, the 20th century, World War II, racial segregation in 1950s' America, and a local history focus.

Children should be taught about:

- *changes within living memory. Where appropriate, these should be used to reveal aspects of change in national life*
  Children learn how telephones have changed, how Guy Fawkes Night celebrations have changed and how life has changed for children since World War II.

- *events beyond living memory that are significant nationally or globally*
  Children learn about the Gunpowder Plot and the reasons for Guy Fawkes Night celebrations, the Great Exhibition in 1851, and events, festivals or celebrations that relate to their own locality.

- *the lives of significant individuals in the past who have contributed to national and international achievements. Some should be used to compare aspects of life in different periods*
  Children learn about the achievements of Alexander Graham Bell, Prince Albert, and Sir Joseph Paxton. They also study and compare the achievements of Rosa Parks and her stand against racial segregation in the 1950s and Elizabeth Fry and her stand against the poor treatment of women prisoners and their children in early 1800s.

- *significant historical events, people and places in their own locality*
  Children get opportunities to learn about their celebrations for Guy Fawkes Night and how World War II affected their local area. The final chapter allows children to study a significant historical event, person or place in their locality in more depth.

Medium-term planning Autumn 1: Telephones

National Curriculum objectives

Children should be taught about:
- changes within living memory. Where appropriate, these should be used to reveal aspects of change in national life
- the lives of significant individuals in the past who have contributed to national and international achievements. Some should be used to compare aspects of life in different periods
- significant historical events, people, places in their own locality
- events beyond living memory that are significant nationally or globally

W	Outcomes	Historical concepts
1	• Know about past communication methods such as letters, telegrams, smoke signals, message sticks and Morse Code. • Can sort photographs or examples of telephones into chronological order.	• Develop an awareness of the past, using common words and phrases relating to the passing of time. • Show where people and events they study fit within a chronological framework. • Identify similarities and differences between ways of life in different periods. • Use a wide vocabulary of everyday historical terms. • Ask and answer questions, choosing and using parts of stories and other sources to show that they know and understand key features of events. • Understand ways in which we find out about the past.
2	• Know who Alexander Graham Bell was and when he lived. • Can understand the reasons why he invented the telephone. • Can experiment with sound vibrations to understand how Bell invented the telephone.	• Develop an awareness of the past. • Show where people and events they study fit within a chronological framework. • Use a wide vocabulary of everyday historical terms. • Choosing and using parts of stories and sources to show that they know and understand key features of events. • Understand ways in which we find out about the past.
3	• Can investigate an old telephone and describe it. • Can make comparisons with a modern telephone. • Can use sources such as photographs and oral accounts to find out about a telephone exchange from the past and how it was used.	• Develop an awareness of the past. • Identify similarities and differences between ways of life in different periods. • Use a wide vocabulary of everyday historical terms. • Choosing and using parts of stories and sources to show that they know and understand key features of events. • Understand ways in which we find out about the past.
4	• Can make simple telephone switchboards and write dialogue for the operator and user. • Can create an old-fashioned telephone exchange for class role play.	• Develop an awareness of the past. • Show where people and events they study fit within a chronological framework. • Identify similarities and differences between ways of life in different periods. • Use a wide vocabulary of everyday historical terms. • Choosing and using parts of stories and sources to show that they know and understand key features of events. • Understand ways in which we find out about the past. • Identify different ways in which the past is represented.
5	• Know when telephone boxes were first used and discuss the change in design over time. • Can write a telephone box poem. • Know how people used telephones in telephone boxes. • Know some reasons why telephone boxes are not used so much today.	• Develop an awareness of the past. • Identify similarities and differences between ways of life in different periods. • Use a wide vocabulary of everyday historical terms. • Choosing and using parts of stories and sources to show that they know and understand key features of events. • Understand ways in which we find out about the past.
6	• Know that emergency services are available by telephone and can recreate emergency scenarios. • Are familiar with the appearance of some unusual telephone designs of the past and can design a telephone of the future.	• (same as week 3)
Assess and review		• To assess the half-term's work.

Medium-term planning Autumn 2: The Gunpowder Plot and Guy Fawkes (Bonfire) Night

National Curriculum objectives

Children should be taught about:
- events beyond living memory that are significant nationally or globally
- the lives of significant individuals in the past who have contributed to national and international achievements. Some should be used to compare aspects of life in different periods

W	Outcomes	Historical concepts
1	• Can link Guy Fawkes Night to the Gunpowder Plot that took place long ago. • Know when and where the Gunpowder Plot took place. • Know that James I was king at the time of the plot, and that this was during the Stuart period. • Aware of the differences between the Catholics and Protestants in Stuart England and why James I upset the Catholics.	• Develop an awareness of the past, using common words and phrases relating to the passing of time. • Show where people and events they study fit within a chronological framework. • Identify similarities and differences between ways of life in different periods. • Use a wide vocabulary of everyday historical terms. • Ask and answer questions, choosing and using parts of stories and other sources to show that they know and understand key features of events. • Understand ways in which we find out about the past. • Identify different ways in which the past is represented.
2	• Can use a range of sources to find out who Guy Fawkes was and what his religious views were. • Can create a short biographical report of his life. • Know about the meeting of the Gunpowder Plot conspirators and the outlines of their plan. • Know what 'Parliament' means and what the 'Opening of Parliament' was.	• Develop an awareness of the past. • Show where people and events they study fit within a chronological framework. • Use a wide vocabulary of everyday historical terms. • Choosing and using parts of stories and sources to show that they know and understand key features of events. • Understand ways in which we find out about the past. • Identify different ways in which the past is represented.
3	• Can study a picture to discuss the image it is trying to create of the eight conspirators. • Can create biographical fact files and pictures for each conspirator. • Can use hot-seat sessions to interview the conspirators and their motives. • Can debate whether the conspirators are right or wrong.	• Show where people and events they study fit within a chronological framework. • Identify similarities and differences between ways of life. • Use a wide vocabulary of everyday historical terms. • Choosing and using parts of stories and sources to show that they know and understand key features of events. • Understand ways in which we find out about the past. • Identify different ways in which the past is represented.
4	• Know that the gunpowder was stored in the cellars of the House of Lords. • Can investigate who might have sent the Monteagle letter and write their own letters of warning to family members. • Can use a range of sources to find out what happened on 5 November 1605. • Can recount the event in the style of a 17th century pamphlet.	• Develop an awareness of the past. • Use a wide vocabulary of everyday historical terms. • Ask and answer questions, choosing and using parts of stories and other sources to show that they know and understand key features of events. • Understand some of the ways in which we find out about the past. • Identify different ways in which the past is represented.
5	• Know about Guy Fawkes' torture and the capture of the other conspirators. • Can discuss why Guy Fawkes is remembered and not the rest of the conspirators. • Can create a newspaper front page report. • Can put the event into chronological order. • Can work in groups to re-enact the plot.	• (same as week 1)
6	• Know why and how people celebrated 5 November in the Stuart period. • Can compare local present-day Guy Fawkes traditions to ones of the past. • Can compose a song about Guy Fawkes Night.	• (same as week 1)
Assess and review		• To assess the half-term's work.

Medium-term planning Spring 1: Women who made a difference (Rosa Parks and Elizabeth Fry)

National Curriculum objectives

Children should be taught about:
- the lives of significant individuals in the past who have contributed to national and international achievements. Some should be used to compare aspects of life in different periods
- changes within living memory. Where appropriate, these should be used to reveal aspects of change in national life.
- events beyond living memory that are significant nationally or globally

W	Outcomes	Historical concepts
1	• Can use sources to find out who Rosa Parks was and when and where she lived. • Know about her children by listening to extracts from her autobiography. • Can use media sources and photographs to understand and discuss what segregation is and how it was used in the USA in the 1950s.	• Develop an awareness of the past. • Show where people and events they study fit within a chronological framework. • Identify similarities and differences between ways of life in different periods. • Use a wide vocabulary of everyday historical terms. • Ask and answer questions, choosing and using parts of stories and other sources to show that they know and understand key features of events. • Understand ways in which we find out about the past. • Identify different ways in which the past is represented.
2	• Know about Rosa Parks' actions on the bus on 1 December 1955. • Can understand how the bus was set out and the rules used for the bus. • Can work in groups to create dialogue for TV or radio interviews with passengers with different viewpoints, about what happened on the bus.	• Develop an awareness of the past. • Identify similarities and differences between ways of life in different periods. • Use a wide vocabulary of everyday historical terms. • Choosing and using parts of stories and sources to show that they know and understand key features of events. • Understand ways in which we find out about the past. • Identify different ways in which the past is represented.
3	• Know about the Montgomery Bus Boycott and can write protest letters. • Can write a short obituary of her life.	• (same as week 2)
4	• Can use sources to find out who Elizabeth Fry was and where and when she lived. • Can draw a portrait of her and a timeline. • Know about prison conditions for women and children in the early 19th century. • Can write illustrated information sheets of what they see as prison visitors.	• Develop an awareness of the past. • Show where people and events they study fit within a chronological framework. • Identify similarities and differences between ways of life in different periods. • Use a wide vocabulary of everyday historical terms. • Choosing and using parts of stories and sources to show that they know and understand key features of events. • Understand ways in which we find out about the past.
5	• Can find out how Elizabeth Fry helped the female prisoners by setting up a school and giving them jobs to do. • Can think of items that Elizabeth Fry could give to the prisoners. • Know the story/folk song of the 'Rajah quilt'. • Know how the convicts created the quilt on the voyage to Australia with Fry's sewing kits. • Can create their own story paper quilts.	• Show where people and events they study fit within a chronological framework. • Identify similarities and differences between ways of life in different periods. • Use a wide vocabulary of everyday historical terms. • Choosing and using parts of stories and sources to show that they know and understand key features of events. • Understand ways in which we find out about the past. • Identify different ways in which the past is represented.
6	• Can compare the ways Rosa Parks and Elizabeth Fry made a difference to other people's lives and how they were criticised by some. • Can discuss and set out plans of how they would like to make a difference to other people's lives.	• Show where people and events they study fit within a chronological framework. • Identify similarities and differences between ways of life in different periods. • Use a wide vocabulary of everyday historical terms. • Choosing and using parts of stories and sources to show that they know and understand key features of events. • Understand ways in which we find out about the past.
Assess and review		• To assess the half-term's work.

Medium-term planning Spring 2: Victorians (the Great Exhibition)

National Curriculum objectives

Children should be taught about:
- events beyond living memory that are significant nationally or globally
- the lives of significant individuals in the past who have contributed to national and international achievements. Some should be used to compare aspects of life in different periods

W	Outcomes	Historical concepts
1	• Can use sources to identify who Queen Victoria and Prince Albert were, when they lived and link this time with the Victorian period. • Know about Prince Albert's idea for the first world trade fair and when and where it was to be held. • Can understand what 'empire' means and link it to the British Empire of Victorian times.	• Develop an awareness of the past. • Show where people and events they study fit within a chronological framework. • Identify similarities and differences between ways of life in different periods. • Use a wide vocabulary of everyday historical terms. • Choosing and using parts of stories and sources to show that they know and understand key features of events. • Understand ways in which we find out about the past.
2	• Can use sources to discover how the exhibition space of the Crystal Palace was planned and built, and why it was called the Crystal Palace. • Can use sources to make a class model of the Crystal Palace.	• Use a wide vocabulary of everyday historical terms. • Ask and answer questions, choosing and using parts of stories and other sources to show that they know and understand key features of events. • Understand ways in which we find out about the past.
3	• Know about the opening ceremony of the Great Exhibition from eye-witness accounts. • Can write a recount of the opening for the front page of a Victorian newspaper. • Can work out what was in the Great Exhibition halls from a range of sources. • Can write a report of the interior.	• Develop an awareness of the past, using common words and phrases relating to the passing of time. • Use a wide vocabulary of everyday historical terms. • Choosing and using parts of stories and sources to show that they know and understand key features of events. • Understand ways in which we find out about the past. • Identify different ways in which the past is represented.
4	• Can understand what an exhibit is. • Can use sources to identify the wide range of exhibits from the United Kingdom. • Can create their own exhibit and write an entry for the catalogue. • Can study pictures to find out about the wide range of exhibit designs. • Can design stands for a role play area.	• Develop an awareness of the past, using common words and phrases relating to the passing of time. • Identify similarities and differences between ways of life in different periods. • Use a wide vocabulary of everyday historical terms. • Choosing and using parts of stories and sources to show that they know and understand key features of events. • Understand ways in which we find out about the past.
5	• Can locate on a map where the international exhibitors came from and understand that for many it was the first time that they had seen people or things from overseas. • Can write an exhibition log book about an international exhibit. • Know that people from the UK were able to visit the Great Exhibition due to 'shilling days'. • Can create local advertisements train trips to the Great Exhibition.	• Identify similarities and differences between ways of life in different periods. • Use a wide vocabulary of everyday historical terms. • Choosing and using parts of stories and sources to show that they know and understand key features of events. • Understand some of the ways in which we find out about the past. • Identify different ways in which the past is represented.
6	• Can use sources to discuss the range of visitors from the UK, and their experiences. • Can use their knowledge of the Great Exhibition to recount a trip to London and visiting the Great Exhibition. • Know what happened to the Crystal Palace after the exhibition. • Design a new Crystal Palace for the future and decide what it could include.	• Develop an awareness of the past. • Show where people and events they study fit within a chronological framework. • Identify similarities and differences between ways of life in different periods. • Use a wide vocabulary of everyday historical terms. • Choosing and using parts of stories and sources to show that they know and understand key features of events. • Understand ways in which we find out about the past. • Identify different ways in which the past is represented.
Assess and review		• To assess the half-term's work.

Medium-term planning Summer 1: What was it like to be a child during World War II?

National Curriculum objectives

Children should be taught about:
• changes within living memory. Where appropriate, these should be used to reveal aspects of change in national life

W	Outcomes	Historical concepts
1	• Know when World War II was and can put it into a timeline. • Can understand what 'rationing' means and know what was rationed. • Can investigate a copy of a ration book to find out about food rationing. • Can compare a World War II meal with a present day meal.	• Develop an awareness of the past, using common words and phrases relating to the passing of time. • Show where people and events they study fit within a chronological framework. • Use a wide vocabulary of everyday historical terms. • Ask and answer questions, choosing and using parts of stories and other sources to show that they know and understand key features of events. • Understand ways in which we find out about the past.
2	• Know why and how people used allotments and window boxes for growing food. • Can create a vegetable growing planner. • Can use 'Dig for Victory' posters for inspiration when designing their own posters to encourage others to grow food.	• Develop an awareness of the past, using common words and phrases relating to the passing of time. • Identify similarities and differences between ways of life in different periods. • Use a wide vocabulary of everyday historical terms. • Ask and answer questions, choosing and using parts of stories and other sources to show that they know and understand key features of events. • Understand ways in which we find out about the past. • Identify different ways in which the past is represented.
3	• Know about clothes rationing and the use of protective clothing such as gas masks. • Can design an outfit from pieces of material. • Have a 'Make do and mend' session using pieces of material. • Can discuss why 'make do and mend' is a good idea.	• Develop an awareness of the past, using common words and phrases relating to the passing of time. • Identify similarities and differences between ways of life in different periods. • Use a wide vocabulary of everyday historical terms. • Ask and answer questions, choosing and using parts of stories and other sources to show that they know and understand key features of events. • Understand ways in which we find out about the past.
4	• Can use sources to understand why and when air raid shelters were used. • Can label a diagram and write a short explanation of an Anderson shelter.	• Develop an awareness of the past. • Use a wide vocabulary of everyday historical terms. • Ask and answer questions, choosing and using parts of stories and other sources to show that they know and understand key features of events. • Understand ways in which we find out about the past.
5	• Can understand the term 'evacuation'. • Know why children were evacuated and what they had to do. • Know what it was like to be an evacuee, from oral accounts. • Can write diary accounts of their own imagined experience.	• Develop an awareness of the past. • Identify similarities and differences between ways of life in different periods. • Use a wide vocabulary of everyday historical terms. • Ask and answer questions, choosing and using parts of stories and other sources to show that they know and understand key features of events. • Understand ways in which we find out about the past. • Identify different ways in which the past is represented.
6	• Can understand what it was like to be an evacuee, by listening to a visitor who experienced being an evacuee or can remember evacuees coming to the area. • Can use their knowledge of evacuation to have a re-enactment drama session. • Can discuss how they felt during the re-enactment.	• (same as week 2)
Assess and review		• To assess the half-term's work.

Medium-term planning Summer 2: Customs, festivals and fairs from around the UK

National Curriculum objectives

Children should be taught about:
- significant historical events, people, places in their own locality
- events beyond living memory that are significant nationally or globally

W	Outcomes	Historical concepts
1	• Can find out what 'well dressing' is and where and when it takes place in the United Kingdom. • Can write a report on the custom. • Can use sources to create a 'well dressing' design based on a well-known local event, story, person or place.	• Develop an awareness of the past, using common words and phrases relating to the passing of time. • Show where people and events they study fit within a chronological framework. • Use a wide vocabulary of everyday historical terms. • Ask and answer questions, choosing and using parts of stories and other sources to show that they know and understand key features of events. • Understand some of the ways in which we find out about the past. • Identify different ways in which the past is represented.
2	• Can locate the National Eisteddfod festival to Wales; they know about its heritage and customs. • Can work in groups to rehearse and perform a class Eisteddfod.	• (same as week 1)
3	• Know that the Highland Games are held in Scotland. • Know about the origins of the games and the different activities. • Have a class Highland Games using a mix of their own choice of old-fashioned and modern-day games.	• Develop an awareness of the past, using common words and phrases relating to the passing of time. • Show where people and events they study fit within a chronological framework. • Identify similarities and differences between ways of life in different periods. • Use a wide vocabulary of everyday historical terms. • Ask and answer questions, choosing and using parts of stories and other sources to show that they know and understand key features of events. • Understand ways in which we find out about the past.
4	• Can identify where and when the Notting Hill Carnival takes place. • Know about its multi-cultural origins and can put the events on a timeline. • Can use sources to look at the features of the carnival. • Can design a carnival mask and headdresses, using recycled materials, for their own carnival.	• (same week 1)
5	• Know some different features and customs of fair days in the United Kingdom. • Know the origins of a fair or custom in their local area. • Can use their knowledge to organise a mini fair or festival centred around a well-known historic event, person or place.	• Develop an awareness of the past, using common words and phrases relating to the passing of time. • Identify similarities and differences between ways of life in different periods. • Use a wide vocabulary of everyday historical terms. • Ask and answer questions, choosing and using parts of stories and other sources to show that they know and understand key features of events. • Understand some of the ways in which we find out about the past. • Identify different ways in which the past is represented.
6	• Can create resources for their mini fair or festival. • Can put on their mini fair or festival for other classes or school visitors.	• (same as week 5)
Assess and review		• To assess the half-term's work.

Year 2 Background knowledge

In the Year 2, there is a varied range of topics that follow the main four curriculum objectives – changes within living memory, events beyond living memory, lives of significant others and significant historical events, people and places in their locality. However, generic history skills should develop as the year progresses, so these have been woven into the content planning. Some of these important history skills and themes are listed below.

An awareness of time and simple chronological frameworks

In Year 2, children continue to use common words and phrases that relate to the passing of time but with more understanding of their meanings. Initially, these can be developed by describing events in their own lives or through recounting stories but they should then progress on to changes in events in recent and distant history. They continue to use chronological sequencing to place objects and pictures into a time sequence. Many of the chronological frameworks within the Year 2 chapters focus on putting short-term events into timeframes using timelines, oral recounts, drama or written recounts, such as the events of the Gunpowder Plot. The historical periods are also put into context with the children being aware that the Gunpowder Plot is in the distant past around the time of the Great Fire of London; and that Rosa Parks lived within living memory, unlike Elizabeth Fry.

Similarity and difference – a sense of the past

One historical skill that can be developed early is children's awareness of similarities and differences in past objects, pictures, stories and events compared to their own lives. In the Year 2 chapters, children get the opportunity to listen to oral accounts, and to investigate written and visual sources and artefacts in more detail to find comparisons with the past and present, such as the history of telephones and the rationing and the evacuation experiences of children during World War II. Re-enactment, role-play and imaginative play help reinforce these skills and develop the children's empathy with people who lived in the past. Children are also able to make more detailed comparisons between different parts of society in one period of history, such as the lives of women prisoners and their children in the 19th century, racial segregation in the USA and the different classes visiting the Great Exhibition.

Cause and consequence

Children go into more detail about the causes of events or reasons why people did things and the changes or consequences they caused in society. For example, in the chapter about Rosa Parks and Elizabeth Fry, children learn why both women decided to make a stand and the consequences for others and for themselves. They also look at the consequences of the actions of the Gunpowder conspirators and the effects still felt today, and reasons behind the Great Exhibition and how the rest of the world saw the United Kingdom as a result.

Asking and answering questions

Children progress from asking and answering simple questions about events or stories from the past, to using different sources of information to be able to make their own enquiries and deduce the answers. These can be encouraged through investigating an Elizabeth Fry artefact bag, or an evacuee's suitcase. Opportunities for imaginative play allow children to take time to role play and to develop their enquiry and empathy skills.

Constructing and interpreting the past from evidence

Children use a wide range of sources to help them construct the past, such as paintings, 17th century pamphlets, photographs, written sources, oral accounts, multimedia, newspaper accounts, stories and rhymes, music, dance, drama, posters, diagrams, exhibition catalogues, class trips and a range of artefacts including telephones and Victorian items. Children start to learn that the past can be interpreted in different ways by discovering that people and accounts have different points of view or experiences. They also get opportunities through drama and filming news reports to show different viewpoints.

Local history focuses

Throughout Year 2, there are opportunities to include a local history focus to enhance the learning experiences of the children. A trip could be arranged to a local telephone exchange; local museums; libraries and museums can give more information about the local area during World War II and older people could be invited to share their wartime memories. In the last chapter, children can find out or use a historic local event, place or person as a focus for their mini festival or fair. This chapter also allows them to find out more about local traditions and customs that may be unique to their area.

Year 3 Long-term planning

1. *Children should know and understand the history of these islands as a coherent, chronological narrative, from the earliest times to the present day: how people's lives have shaped this nation and how Britain has influenced and been influenced by the wider world.*

   Within the Year 3 chapters, children begin to learn about the chronological narrative of Britain's history, exploring it from the Stone Age, through the Bronze Age to the Iron Age. They then move to the wider world, gaining an overview of when and where the earliest civilisations were before embarking on a depth study of the ancient Egyptians.

2. *Children should know and understand significant aspects of the history of the wider world: the nature of ancient civilisations; the expansion and dissolution of empires; characteristic features of past non-European societies; achievements and follies of mankind.*

   Within the Year 3 chapters, children will cover the ancient civilisation of Egypt, its characteristics and achievements (including the pyramids, hieroglyphics, art, artefacts, pharaohs, mummification and mythology).

3. *Children should gain and deploy a historically grounded understanding of abstract terms such as 'empire', 'civilisation', 'parliament' and 'peasantry'.*

   Within Year 3, children develop their understanding of a variety of such terms (including 'settlers', 'civilisation', 'slavery', 'status', 'power', 'primitive' and 'Neolithic').

4. *Children should understand historical concepts such as continuity and change, cause and consequence, similarity, difference and significance, and use them to make connections, draw contrasts, analyse trends, frame historically valid questions and create their own structured accounts, including written narratives and analyses.*

   Within all six Year 3 chapters, children are given the opportunity to learn about the above historical concepts and use them in the ways described. At the end of the year, children complete an independent project in which they devise, research, analyse and answer a historically valid question of their choice.

5. *Children should understand the methods of historical enquiry, including how evidence is used rigorously to make historical claims, and discern how and why contrasting arguments and interpretations of the past have been constructed.*

   Within the Year 3 chapters, children are introduced to historical enquiry and interpretations of the past via written and archaeological evidence, as well as artefacts. This provides grounding for later years, in which they move on to examine evidence more critically and understand that this can be interpreted in a number of ways.

6. *Children should gain historical perspective by placing their growing knowledge into different contexts, understanding the connections between local, regional, national and international history; between cultural, economic, military, political, religious and social history; and between short- and long-term timescales.*

   Within the Year 3 chapters, children begin to understand the difference between national and international history, studying first the early history of Britain and then looking at the wider world during a similar time period. They consider a variety of aspects for each civilisation they study, including culture, art, burial, beliefs, archaeological findings, homes, weapons and mythology. They also look at timescales from their own lives to the achievements of civilisations over hundreds of years.

Overview of progression in Year 3

Children should continue to develop a chronologically secure knowledge and understanding of British, local and world history, establishing clear narratives within and across the periods they study. They should note connections, contrasts and trends over time and develop the appropriate use of historical terms. They should regularly address and sometimes devise historically valid questions about change, cause, similarity and difference, and significance. They should construct informed responses that involve thoughtful selection and organisation of relevant historical information. They should understand how our knowledge of the past is constructed from a range of sources and that different versions of past events may exist, giving some reasons for this.

In planning to ensure the progression described above through teaching the British, local and world history outlined below, teachers should combine overview and depth studies to help children understand both the long arc of development and the complexity of specific aspects of the content.

Children should be taught about:

- *changes in Britain from the Stone Age to the Iron Age*

In the Year 3 chapters, children will learn about:

- Stone Age tools and weapons, cave art and early farming
- Bronze Age metalworking technology, round barrows, roundhouses and Stonehenge
- Iron Age tribal kingdoms, warriors and weaponry, hill forts, technology, druids, farming and trade, artwork and crafts.

- *the achievements of the earliest civilisations – an overview of where and when the first civilisations appeared and a depth study of ancient Egypt*
  In Year 3, children study the Egyptians, including the pyramids, the Rosetta Stone, hieroglyphics, wall art, the discovery of Tutankhamen's tomb, famous Egyptians, mummification, the myth of Osiris and Seth and the importance of the Nile.

Overview and depth studies

The planning incorporates both overview studies and depth studies, but you may choose to adapt lessons to focus on certain topics in more detail or to skip lessons to shorten topics.

Depth studies could include the following:

Autumn 1: providing food (hunter-gatherer lifestyle versus farming); why Skara Brae is important for historians

Autumn 2: considering the mystery of why and how Stonehenge was built and why it is an important landmark

Spring 1: why it was important for the Celtic tribes to protect themselves and how they did this

Spring 2: Celtic art and jewellery designs; the mystery of who the druids were and what they looked like; life in an Iron Age hill fort

Summer 1: answering historical questions about the pyramids; the story of Tutankhamen and the discovery of his tomb

Summer 2: Egyptian gods and goddesses, mythology and belief about the afterlife

Note: the outcomes, objectives and concepts outlined in the medium-term planning grids for each week are spread across two lessons

Medium-term planning Autumn 1: History skills/ The Stone Age

National Curriculum objective

Children should be taught about:
• the changes in Britain from the Stone Age to the Iron Age

W	Outcomes	Historical concepts
1	• Can understand how evidence is used to give us a picture of life in the past. • Can understand why contrasting interpretations of the past have been constructed.	• Understand how our knowledge of the past is constructed from a range of sources. • Understand that different versions of past events may exist, giving some reasons for this.
2	• Can create a simple timeline showing events in their own or a family member's life. • Can describe how timelines are used and can identify short- and long-term timescales.	• Develop the appropriate use of historical terms. • Construct informed responses that involve thoughtful selection and organisation of relevant historical information.
3	• Can locate the different periods of the Stone Age on a timeline. • Can describe the hunter-gatherer life of the late Neolithic period.	• Develop a chronologically secure knowledge and understanding of British, local and world history, establishing clear narratives within and across the periods they study. • Develop the appropriate use of historical terms.
4	• Can describe Stone Age tools and weaponry. • Can consider how Skara Brae gives us a picture of Stone Age life.	• Develop a chronologically secure knowledge and understanding of British, local and world history, establishing clear narratives within and across the periods they study. • Develop the appropriate use of historical terms. • Understand how our knowledge of the past is constructed from a range of sources. • Understand that different versions of past events may exist, giving some reasons for this.
5	• Can use online information to write facts about Skara Brae. • Can create their own cave paintings.	• Develop a chronologically secure knowledge and understanding of British, local and world history, establishing clear narratives within and across the periods they study. • Develop the appropriate use of historical terms. • Understand how our knowledge of the past is constructed from a range of sources. • Understand that different versions of past events may exist, giving some reasons for this.
6	• Can describe the development of early farming in Britain. • Can compare the hunter-gatherer and farming lifestyles.	• Develop a chronologically secure knowledge and understanding of British, local and world history, establishing clear narratives within and across the periods they study. • Note connections, contrasts and trends over time. • Develop the appropriate use of historical terms. • Regularly address and sometimes devise historically valid questions about change, cause, similarity and difference, and significance. • Construct informed responses that involve thoughtful selection and organisation of relevant historical information.
Assess and review		• To assess the half-term's work.

Medium-term planning Autumn 2: The Bronze Age

National Curriculum objective

Children should be taught about:
- the changes in Britain from the Stone Age to the Iron Age

W	Outcomes	Historical concepts
1	• Can show the relationship between the Stone, Bronze and Iron Ages on a timeline. • Can describe how technology helps historians study the past.	• Develop a chronologically secure knowledge and understanding of British, local and world history, establishing clear narratives within and across the periods they study. • Note connections, contrasts and trends over time. • Develop the appropriate use of historical terms. • Regularly address and sometimes devise historically valid questions about change, cause, similarity and difference, and significance. • Construct informed responses that involve thoughtful selection and organisation of relevant historical information. • Understand how our knowledge of the past is constructed from a range of sources. • Understand that different versions of past events may exist, giving some reasons for this.
2	• Can use evidence to make inferences about the Bronze Age. • Can describe how the immigration of the Beaker People started the Bronze Age in Britain.	• (same as week 1)
3	• Can describe a Bronze Age roundhouse. • Can describe what bell beaker pottery was like.	• Develop a chronologically secure knowledge and understanding of British, local and world history, establishing clear narratives within and across the periods they study. • Regularly address and sometimes devise historically valid questions about change, cause, similarity and difference, and significance. • Construct informed responses that involve thoughtful selection and organisation of relevant historical information. • Understand how our knowledge of the past is constructed from a range of sources. • Understand that different versions of past events may exist, giving some reasons for this.
4	• Can understand how burial rituals changed from the Stone Age (long barrows) to the Bronze Age (round barrows). • Can write about a day in the life of a Bronze Age person.	• Develop a chronologically secure knowledge and understanding of British, local and world history, establishing clear narratives within and across the periods they study. • Note connections, contrasts and trends over time and develop the appropriate use of historical terms. • Regularly address and sometimes devise historically valid questions about change, cause, similarity and difference, and significance. • Understand how our knowledge of the past is constructed from a range of sources.
5	• Can describe why opinions about the origins of Stonehenge differ. • Can use diagrams to create their own model of Stonehenge.	• Develop a chronologically secure knowledge and understanding of British, local and world history, establishing clear narratives within and across the periods they study. • Understand how our knowledge of the past is constructed from a range of sources. • Understand that different versions of past events may exist, giving some reasons for this.
6	• Can describe why Stonehenge is a significant landmark. • Can describe the main changes in Britain from the Stone Age to the Bronze Age.	• (same as week 3)
Assess and review		• To assess the half-term's work.

Medium-term planning Spring 1: The Iron Age (Celts)

National Curriculum objective

Children should be taught about:
- the changes in Britain from the Stone Age to the Iron Age

W	Outcomes	Historical concepts
1	• Can describe some of the main Celtic tribes. • Can locate the main tribal kingdoms.	• Develop a chronologically secure knowledge and understanding of British, local and world history, establishing clear narratives within and across the periods they study. • Regularly address and sometimes devise historically valid questions about change, cause, similarity and difference, and significance.
2	• Can make inferences about Iron Age life from the finds of the Llyn Cerrig Bach hoard. • Can describe the Celts' appearance.	• Develop a chronologically secure knowledge and understanding of British, local and world history, establishing clear narratives within and across the periods they study. • Construct informed responses that involve thoughtful selection and organisation of relevant historical information. • Understand how our knowledge of the past is constructed from a range of sources. • Understand that different versions of past events may exist, giving some reasons for this.
3	• Can describe Celtic warfare and weaponry.	• Develop a chronologically secure knowledge and understanding of British, local and world history, establishing clear narratives within and across the periods they study. • Develop the appropriate use of historical terms. • Understand how our knowledge of the past is constructed from a range of sources. • Understand that different versions of past events may exist, giving some reasons for this.
4	• Can describe Iron Age dwellings. • Can describe Iron Age hill forts.	• Develop a chronologically secure knowledge and understanding of British, local and world history, establishing clear narratives within and across the periods they study. • Note connections, contrasts and trends over time and develop the appropriate use of historical terms. • Regularly address and sometimes devise historically valid questions about change, cause, similarity and difference, and significance. • Construct informed responses that involve thoughtful selection and organisation of relevant historical information. • Understand how our knowledge of the past is constructed from a range of sources.
5	• Can create a model of a hill fort.	• (same as week 4)
6	• Can describe the benefits of Iron Age advances in technology.	• Develop a chronologically secure knowledge and understanding of British, local and world history, establishing clear narratives within and across the periods they study. • Note connections, contrasts and trends over time. • Regularly address and sometimes devise historically valid questions about change, cause, similarity and difference, and significance. • Construct informed responses that involve thoughtful selection and organisation of relevant historical information.
Assess and review		• To assess the half-term's work.

Medium-term planning Spring 2: Celtic culture

National Curriculum objective

Children should be taught about:
• the changes in Britain from the Stone Age to the Iron Age

W	Outcomes	Historical concepts
1	• Can describe ways that Lindow Man provides evidence of Iron Age life. • Can describe Celtic religion and the role of the Druids.	• Develop a chronologically secure knowledge and understanding of British, local and world history, establishing clear narratives within and across the periods they study. • Understand how our knowledge of the past is constructed from a range of sources. • Understand that different versions of past events may exist, giving some reasons for this.
2	• Can describe a druid artefact. • Can describe Iron Age farming and trade.	• Develop a chronologically secure knowledge and understanding of British, local and world history, establishing clear narratives within and across the periods they study. • Regularly address and sometimes devise historically valid questions about change, cause, similarity and difference, and significance. • Understand how our knowledge of the past is constructed from a range of sources. • Understand that different versions of past events may exist, giving some reasons for this.
3	• Can understand how the Celtic calendar was structured. • Can weave and can describe its importance to the Celts.	• Develop a chronologically secure knowledge and understanding of British, local and world history, establishing clear narratives within and across the periods they study. • Regularly address and sometimes devise historically valid questions about change, cause, similarity and difference, and significance. • Understand how our knowledge of the past is constructed from a range of sources.
4	• Can sketch examples of Celtic art and jewellery. • Can create their own Celtic style jewellery.	• Develop a chronologically secure knowledge and understanding of British, local and world history, establishing clear narratives within and across the periods they study. • Understand how our knowledge of the past is constructed from a range of sources.
5	• Can identify Celtic place names in Britain today. • Visit an Iron Age site in their local area (option to research one online if this isn't possible).	• Develop a chronologically secure knowledge and understanding of British, local and world history, establishing clear narratives within and across the periods they study. • Understand how our knowledge of the past is constructed from a range of sources.
6	• Can describe changes in Britain from the Stone Age to the Iron Age.	• Develop a chronologically secure knowledge and understanding of British, local and world history, establishing clear narratives within and across the periods they study. • Regularly address and sometimes devise historically valid questions about change, cause, similarity and difference, and significance. • Understand how our knowledge of the past is constructed from a range of sources. • Understand that different versions of past events may exist, giving some reasons for this.
Assess and review		• To assess the half-term's work.

Medium-term planning Summer 1: Ancient Egypt (1)

National Curriculum objective

Children should be taught about:
• the achievements of the earliest civilisations – an overview of where and when the first civilisations appeared and a depth study of one of the following: ancient Sumer; the Indus Valley; ancient Egypt; the Shang Dynasty of ancient China

W	Outcomes	Historical concepts
1	• Can use maps to identify where the earliest civilisations appeared. • Can use timelines to identify when the earliest civilisations appeared.	• Develop a chronologically secure knowledge and understanding of British, local and world history, establishing clear narratives within and across the periods they study. • Regularly address and sometimes devise historically valid questions about change, cause, similarity and difference, and significance.
2	• Can describe Egyptian social structure. • Can create some Egyptian-style jewellery.	• Develop a chronologically secure knowledge and understanding of British, local and world history, establishing clear narratives within and across the periods they study. • Develop the appropriate use of historical terms.
3	• Can understand how the discovery of the Rosetta Stone led to the deciphering of Egyptian hieroglyphics. • Can recreate some Egyptian hieroglyphs.	• Develop a chronologically secure knowledge and understanding of British, local and world history, establishing clear narratives within and across the periods they study. • Regularly address and sometimes devise historically valid questions about change, cause, similarity and difference, and significance. • Understand how our knowledge of the past is constructed from a range of sources.
4	• Can describe what is known about why and how the great pyramids were built. • Can create a model of the Great Pyramid at Giza.	• Develop a chronologically secure knowledge and understanding of British, local and world history, establishing clear narratives within and across the periods they study. • Understand how our knowledge of the past is constructed from a range of sources.
5	• Can describe the achievements of some famous Egyptians. • Can describe the significance of Howard Carter's discovery of Tutankhamen's tomb.	• Develop a chronologically secure knowledge and understanding of British, local and world history, establishing clear narratives within and across the periods they study. • Regularly address and sometimes devise historically valid questions about change, cause, similarity and difference, and significance. • Understand that different versions of past events may exist, giving some reasons for this.
6	• Can describe artefacts from Tutankhamen's burial treasure and how they were used. • Can create an artwork based on Tutankhamen's death mask.	• Develop a chronologically secure knowledge and understanding of British, local and world history, establishing clear narratives within and across the periods they study. • Regularly address and sometimes devise historically valid questions about change, cause, similarity and difference, and significance. • Understand how our knowledge of the past is constructed from a range of sources. • Understand that different versions of past events may exist, giving some reasons for this.
Assess and review		• To assess the half-term's work.

Medium-term planning Summer 2: Ancient Egypt (2)

National Curriculum objective

Children should be taught about:
- the achievements of the earliest civilisations – an overview of where and when the first civilisations appeared and a depth study of one of the following: ancient Sumer; the Indus Valley; ancient Egypt; the Shang Dynasty of ancient China

W	Outcomes	Historical concepts
1	• Can describe some of the different gods and goddesses worshipped by the Egyptians. • Can describe the story of Osiris and Seth.	• Develop a chronologically secure knowledge and understanding of British, local and world history, establishing clear narratives within and across the periods they study. • Regularly address and sometimes devise historically valid questions about change, cause, similarity and difference, and significance.
2	• Can recreate the story of Osiris and Seth. • Can describe Egyptian beliefs about life after death.	• Develop a chronologically secure knowledge and understanding of British, local and world history, establishing clear narratives within and across the periods they study. • Regularly address and sometimes devise historically valid questions about change, cause, similarity and difference, and significance. • Understand how our knowledge of the past is constructed from a range of sources.
3	• Can describe the mummification process. • Can make their own canopic jars.	• Develop a chronologically secure knowledge and understanding of British, local and world history, establishing clear narratives within and across the periods they study. • Regularly address and sometimes devise historically valid questions about change, cause, similarity and difference, and significance. • Understand how our knowledge of the past is constructed from a range of sources.
4	• Can describe some of the features of Egyptian art. • Can create their own examples of Egyptian pictures.	• Develop a chronologically secure knowledge and understanding of British, local and world history, establishing clear narratives within and across the periods they study. • Regularly address and sometimes devise historically valid questions about change, cause, similarity and difference, and significance.
5	• Can describe why the Nile was important to ancient Egyptians. • Can create a presentation about an aspect of Egyptian life.	• Develop a chronologically secure knowledge and understanding of British, local and world history, establishing clear narratives within and across the periods they study. • Regularly address and sometimes devise historically valid questions about change, cause, similarity and difference, and significance. • Construct informed responses that involve thoughtful selection and organisation of relevant historical information. • Understand how our knowledge of the past is constructed from a range of sources.
6	• Can present their own information about an aspect of Egyptian life.	• (same as week 5)
Assess and review		• To assess the half-term's work.

Year 3 Background knowledge

The Year 3 content begins the chronological narrative of Britain's history, exploring the different cultures which have been established here during the Stone, Bronze and Iron Ages. Children are also introduced to international history as they explore when and where the earliest civilisations took place and then study the ancient Egyptians in detail. In Year 4, they will consolidate their knowledge of the Celts, considering the impact of Roman rule on their culture.

The planning incorporates both overview topics (such as Egyptian mythology) and depth studies (such as the myth of Osiris and Seth, and Egyptian belief about the afterlife), but you may choose to adapt lessons to focus on certain topics in more detail or to skip lessons to shorten topics. While topics follow the chronological history of Britain and the wider world, core history skills should develop as children progress through the different topics; these have been woven into the content planning. Some of these history skills and themes are listed below.

Understanding chronology and timelines

In Year 3, children move from basic division of time into past and present to developing an understanding of the order or chronology of different time periods, considering the changes in Britain from the Stone Age (from the end of the Ice Age around 12,000BC to around 2000BC) to the Bronze Age (from around 2000BC to around 650BC) and then to the Iron Age (from around 650BC to the Roman invasion in AD43). During the topics, children are given opportunity to progress their skills in interpreting and constructing basic timelines to show when significant events occurred, beginning with their own lifespan then moving to long-term timescales following changes in ages over thousands of years.

Addressing and devising historically valid questions

The ability to ask and find answers to questions is a key skill for any historian. In every topic, children have many opportunities to address historically valid questions (for example, How did farming develop in Britain? Why was Stonehenge built? What did the Druids look like? What did the Egyptians believe about the afterlife?) using a range of reliable sources to find answers. Particularly when using the internet, it is important that children understand the difference between a reliable and non-reliable source of information and between fact and opinion. At the end of the year, children are given the opportunity to devise their own historically valid questions and carry out an independent investigation into an area of personal interest on the topic of ancient Egypt (for example, What did the Egyptians eat? How were the pyramids built?), sharing their findings through a project or presentation.

Constructing and interpreting the past from evidence

As children progress as historians they view the past less in terms of facts and more as knowledge constructed from evidence. This evidence could be written (myths recorded in Egyptian hieroglyphics), taken from archaeological sites (Skara Brae, Stonehenge, Iron Age hill forts and the pyramids at Giza), or exist as artefacts (Stone Age tools, the treasures of Tutankhamen's tomb).

Understanding cause, consequence and significance

In the different topics, children have opportunities to start to develop their understanding of the ideas of cause, consequence and significance. For example, they might consider the development of new, metal tools as a consequence of the introduction of metals like bronze to Britain. Significance is explored more fully by the older age groups but can be understood in terms of important historical people or events that we remember for a particular reason, such as bringing about change.

Drawing comparisons

This skill becomes more developed in the older age groups but in Year 3 there are some opportunities for children to think about basic similarities and differences between past civilisations (for example, differences in burial customs, tools and weaponry).

Analysing change and trends over time

In Year 3, this is done on a basic level with children considering some of the things that changed in Britain from age to age (for example, the advances in tools and weapons as new materials like bronze became available). This provides grounding for more detailed analysis of historical trends in the older age groups.

Year 4 Long-term planning

1. *Children should know and understand the history of these islands as a coherent, chronological narrative, from the earliest times to the present day: how people's lives have shaped this nation and how Britain has influenced and been influenced by the wider world.*
   In Year 4, children continue the chronological narrative of Britain's history, looking at the impact of the Roman invasion and settlement of Britain. They also explore the legacy of both the Romans and ancient Greeks and their influence on British life today.

2. *Children should know and understand significant aspects of the history of the wider world: the nature of ancient civilisations; the expansion and dissolution of empires; characteristic features of past non-European societies; achievements and follies of mankind.*
   Children cover the ancient civilisations of Rome and Greece, considering the reasons for the expansion of the Roman Empire and achievements of Romans and Greeks.

3. *Children should gain and deploy a historically-grounded understanding of abstract terms such as 'empire', 'civilisation', 'parliament' and 'peasantry'.*
   Within Year 4, children develop their understanding of a wide variety of such terms, such as 'empire', 'invaders', 'settlers', 'civilisation', 'bias', 'slavery', 'status', 'impact', 'consequence'.

4. *Children should understand historical concepts such as continuity and change, cause and consequence, similarity, difference and significance, and use them to make connections, draw contrasts, analyse trends, frame historically valid questions and create their own structured accounts, including written narratives and analyses.*
   Children are given the opportunity to learn about the above historical concepts and use them in the ways described. They will complete an independent project in which they devise, research, analyse and answer a historically valid question of their choice.

5. *Children should understand the methods of historical enquiry, including how evidence is used rigorously to make historical claims, and discern how and why contrasting arguments and interpretations of the past have been constructed.*
   Within the Year 4 chapters, children are introduced to historical enquiry and interpretations of the past via written and archaeological evidence, as well as artefacts and eyewitness reports. They are encouraged to consider potential bias in different sources of information.

6. *Children should gain historical perspective by placing their growing knowledge into different contexts, understanding the connections between local, regional, national and international history; between cultural, economic, military, political, religious and social history; and between short- and long-term timescales.*
   Children explore the connections between national and international history, studying the Romans both in Rome and in Roman Britain to consider their impact on different regions. They have the opportunity to explore a Roman site in the local region, if accessible. They study each ancient civilisation in terms of culture, art, architecture, military strategy, religion and mythology, social structure and government. They look at timescales from events lasting a few weeks to the achievements of civilisations over hundreds of years.

Overview and depth studies

The planning incorporates both overview studies and depth studies, but you may choose to adapt lessons to focus on certain topics in more detail or to skip lessons to shorten topics. Depth studies could include the following:

Autumn 1: features of Greek architecture; achievements and impact of famous Greeks

Autumn 2: Greek gods and goddesses and mythological creatures; the importance of theatre to the Greeks

Spring 1: the Olympic Games in ancient Greece and its legacy today

Spring 2: the strength of the Roman army, its soldiers, armour, weapons and military tactics; the importance of written and archaeological evidence from Pompeii in helping us to learn about the ancient Romans

Summer 1: Boudica's appearance, personality and achievements and the causes and consequences of the Iceni revolt

Summer 2: the way that Britain was modernised by Roman technology, such as roads, towns, sanitation and aqueducts

Overview of progression in Year 4

Year 4 children should continue to develop a chronologically secure knowledge and understanding of British, local and world history, establishing clear narratives within and across the periods they study. They should note connections, contrasts and trends over time and develop the appropriate use of historical terms. They should regularly address and sometimes devise historically valid questions about change, cause, similarity and difference, and significance. They should construct informed responses that involve thoughtful selection and organisation of relevant historical information. They should understand how our knowledge of the past is constructed from a range of sources and that different versions of past events may exist, giving some reasons for this.

In planning to ensure the progression described above through teaching the British, local and world history outlined below, teachers should combine overview and depth studies to help children understand both the long arc of development and the complexity of specific aspects of the content.

Children should be taught about:

- *Ancient Greece – a study of Greek life and achievements and their influence on the western world*
  Within the three Year 4 chapters covering ancient Greece, children will learn about life in ancient Greece (domestic life, school, clothing, religion and mythology) and Greek achievement and influence (architecture, democracy, military strength, famous Greeks, art, theatre, philosophy and Aesop's fables).

- *the Roman Empire and its impact on Britain*

  The Year 4 material includes lessons on:
  - Julius Caesar's attempted invasion in 55–54BC;
  - the Roman Empire by AD42 and the power of its army (including Roman social structure, leisure, lifestyle, buildings, homes, art, mythology, soldiers, weapons, military strategies and Pompeii);
  - the successful invasion by Claudius and conquest, including Hadrian's Wall and Vindolanda Fort;
  - British resistance (Boudica and Caratacus);
  - the 'Romanisation' of Britain, including sites such as Caerwent, Wroxeter and the Roman baths at Bath and the impact of technology (aqueducts, roads, towns), culture (local government and public entertainment) and beliefs (including early Christianity).

- *a study of an aspect or theme in British history that extends pupils chronological knowledge beyond 1066*
  Within the Year 4 chapters covering the Romans, children will learn about the impact and legacy of the Romans in Britain (sanitation, coins, leisure, roads, towns and architecture). In the chapter dedicated to the legacy of the Greeks, children explore Greek influence on modern theatre, science and medicine, sculpture through the ages, architecture, our democratic system, philosophy, the English language, Pythagoras' theorem and the Olympic Games.

Note: the outcomes, objectives and concepts outlined in the medium-term planning grids for each week are spread across two lessons

■SCHOLASTIC

Medium-term planning Autumn 1: Life in ancient Greece

National Curriculum objective

Children should be taught about:
• Ancient Greece – a study of Greek life and achievements and their influence on the western world

W	Outcomes	Historical concepts
1	• Know when and where the civilisation of ancient Greece took place. • Can describe Greek clothing and hairstyles.	• Develop a chronologically secure knowledge and understanding of British, local and world history, establishing clear narratives within and across the periods they study. • Develop the appropriate use of historical terms. • Regularly address and sometimes devise historically valid questions about change, cause, similarity and difference, and significance.
2	• Can compare Greek domestic life with today. • Can compare the Greek alphabet to our own.	• Develop a chronologically secure knowledge and understanding of British, local and world history, establishing clear narratives within and across the periods they study. • Regularly address and sometimes devise historically valid questions about change, cause, similarity and difference, and significance.
3	• Can describe the Acropolis of Athens. • Can design a Greek-style column.	• Develop a chronologically secure knowledge and understanding of British, local and world history, establishing clear narratives within and across the periods they study. • Understand how our knowledge of the past is constructed from a range of sources.
4	• Can debate the pros and cons of the removal of the Elgin Marbles from the Parthenon. • Can compare the lives of people in Athens and Sparta.	• Develop a chronologically secure knowledge and understanding of British, local and world history, establishing clear narratives within and across the periods they study. • Note connections, contrasts and trends over time and develop the appropriate use of historical terms. • Regularly address and sometimes devise historically valid questions about change, cause, similarity and difference, and significance. • Construct informed responses that involve thoughtful selection and organisation of relevant historical information. • Understand that different versions of past events may exist, giving some reasons for this.
5	• Can describe some main events of the Persian Wars. • Can retell the story of the Trojan Horse.	• Develop a chronologically secure knowledge and understanding of British, local and world history, establishing clear narratives within and across the periods they study. • Understand how our knowledge of the past is constructed from a range of sources.
6	• Can describe the achievements of some famous Greeks. • Can debate which Greek made the biggest impact.	• Develop a chronologically secure knowledge and understanding of British, local and world history, establishing clear narratives within and across the periods they study. • Regularly address and sometimes devise historically valid questions about change, cause, similarity and difference, and significance. • Understand how our knowledge of the past is constructed from a range of sources. • Understand that different versions of past events may exist, giving some reasons for this.
Assess and review		• To assess the half-term's work.

Medium-term planning Autumn 2: Ancient Greek culture

YEAR 4

National Curriculum objective

Children should be taught about:
● Ancient Greece – a study of Greek life and achievements and their influence on the western world

W	Outcomes	Historical concepts
1	● Can describe some of the different gods and goddesses worshipped by the Greeks. ● Can consider the characteristics of the Greek gods and goddesses.	● Develop a chronologically secure knowledge and understanding of British, local and world history, establishing clear narratives within and across the periods they study. ● Regularly address and sometimes devise historically valid questions about change, cause, similarity and difference, and significance.
2	● Can describe the myth of Perseus and Medusa. ● Can devise a performance using dance and movement to portray a Greek myth.	● Develop a chronologically secure knowledge and understanding of British, local and world history, establishing clear narratives within and across the periods they study. ● Regularly address and sometimes devise historically valid questions about change, cause, similarity and difference, and significance. ● Understand how our knowledge of the past is constructed from a range of sources.
3	● Can describe the myth of Hades and Persephone. ● Can create a piece of art depicting a mythological creature.	● Develop a chronologically secure knowledge and understanding of British, local and world history, establishing clear narratives within and across the periods they study. ● Regularly address and sometimes devise historically valid questions about change, cause, similarity and difference, and significance. ● Understand how our knowledge of the past is constructed from a range of sources.
4	● Can explore some of Aesop's fables through drama. ● Can discuss the moral of some of Aesop's fables.	● Develop a chronologically secure knowledge and understanding of British, local and world history, establishing clear narratives within and across the periods they study. ● Regularly address and sometimes devise historically valid questions about change, cause, similarity and difference, and significance. ● Understand how our knowledge of the past is constructed from a range of sources.
5	● Can describe ancient Greek pottery artefacts. ● Can create a piece of art in the style of ancient Greek pottery.	● Develop a chronologically secure knowledge and understanding of British, local and world history, establishing clear narratives within and across the periods they study. ● Regularly address and sometimes devise historically valid questions about change, cause, similarity and difference, and significance. ● Understand how our knowledge of the past is constructed from a range of sources.
6	● Can describe what ancient Greek theatres were like. ● Can create Greek-style theatre masks.	● Develop a chronologically secure knowledge and understanding of British, local and world history, establishing clear narratives within and across the periods they study. ● Regularly address and sometimes devise historically valid questions about change, cause, similarity and difference, and significance. ● Understand how our knowledge of the past is constructed from a range of sources.
Assess and review		● To assess the half-term's work.

Medium-term planning Spring 1: The legacy of the ancient Greeks

National Curriculum objective

Children should be taught about:
- Ancient Greece – a study of Greek life and achievements and their influence on the western world
- a study of an aspect or theme in British history that extends pupils' chronological knowledge beyond 1066

W	Outcome	Historical concepts
1	• Can read an excerpt of an ancient Greek play. • Can describe some Greek contributions to science and medicine.	• Develop a chronologically secure knowledge and understanding of British, local and world history, establishing clear narratives within and across the periods they study. • Note connections, contrasts and trends over time. • Regularly address and sometimes devise historically valid questions about change, cause, similarity and difference, and significance. • Construct informed responses that involve thoughtful selection and organisation of relevant historical information. • Understand how our knowledge of the past is constructed from a range of sources.
2	• Can identify examples of Greek architecture in modern buildings. • Can describe how democracy began in ancient Athens.	• (same as Week 1)
3	• Can investigate Pythagoras' Theorem. • Know some of the ideas of ancient Greek philosophers.	• (same as week 1)
4	• Can discuss how Greek myths have influenced modern stories and films. • Can use Greek myths as inspiration for their own writing.	• (same as week 1)
5	• Can name English words that are derived from ancient Greek. • Can describe the Olympic Games in ancient Greece.	• (same as week 1)
6	• Can compare the ancient Greek Olympics with those in the modern day. • Can participate in a Greek-style Olympic Games.	• (same as week 1)
Assess and review		• To assess the half-term's work.

Medium-term planning Spring 2: Rome and its Empire

YEAR 4

National Curriculum objective

Children should be taught about:
• the Roman Empire and its impact on Britain

W	Outcomes	Historical concepts
1	• Know when and where the Roman Empire took place. • Can describe some famous buildings in ancient Rome and consider their purpose.	• Develop a chronologically secure knowledge and understanding of British, local and world history, establishing clear narratives within and across the periods they study. • Develop the appropriate use of historical terms. • Regularly address and sometimes devise historically valid questions about change, cause, similarity and difference, and significance. • Understand how our knowledge of the past is constructed from a range of sources.
2	• Can describe the main features of a Roman villa. • Can consider similarities and differences between Roman home life and home life today.	• Develop a chronologically secure knowledge and understanding of British, local and world history, establishing clear narratives within and across the periods they study. • Note connections, contrasts and trends over time. • Regularly address and sometimes devise historically valid questions about change, cause, similarity and difference, and significance.
3	• Can demonstrate understanding of a Roman leisure activity. • Can describe some of the different gods and goddesses worshipped by the Romans.	• Develop a chronologically secure knowledge and understanding of British, local and world history, establishing clear narratives within and across the periods they study. • Note connections, contrasts and trends over time • Develop the appropriate use of historical terms. • Regularly address and sometimes devise historically valid questions about change, cause, similarity and difference, and significance. • Construct informed responses that involve thoughtful selection and organisation of relevant historical information.
4	• Can describe what life was like for a Roman soldier, describing some of the army tactics used. • Can describe some of the weapons used by the Roman army.	• Develop a chronologically secure knowledge and understanding of British, local and world history, establishing clear narratives within and across the periods they study. • Develop the appropriate use of historical terms.
5	• Can identify similarities and differences between Roman and modern coins. • Can create a piece of Roman-style artwork.	• Develop a chronologically secure knowledge and understanding of British, local and world history, establishing clear narratives within and across the periods they study. • Note connections, contrasts and trends over time and develop the appropriate use of historical terms. • Regularly address and sometimes devise historically valid questions about change, cause, similarity and difference, and significance. • Understand how our knowledge of the past is constructed from a range of sources.
6	• Can describe what happened to Pompeii in AD79. • Can describe how knowledge of Roman life has been constructed from Pompeii's archaeological site.	• Develop a chronologically secure knowledge and understanding of British, local and world history, establishing clear narratives within and across the periods they study. • Regularly address and sometimes devise historically valid questions about change, cause, similarity and difference, and significance. • Understand how our knowledge of the past is constructed from a range of sources.
Assess and review		• To assess the half-term's work.

SCHOLASTIC

Medium-term planning Summer 1: Roman Britain (1)

National Curriculum objective

Children should be taught about:
- the Roman Empire and its impact on Britain

W	Outcomes	Historical concepts
1	• Can draw comparisons between Celtic and Roman life. • Can compare and contrast the Celtic warriors with the Roman army.	• Develop a chronologically secure knowledge and understanding of British, local and world history, establishing clear narratives within and across the periods they study. • Note connections, contrasts and trends over time and develop the appropriate use of historical terms. • Regularly address and sometimes devise historically valid questions about change, cause, similarity and difference, and significance.
2	• Can create a timeline showing important events in Roman Britain. • Can identify reasons why the Romans invaded Britain.	• Develop a chronologically secure knowledge and understanding of British, local and world history, establishing clear narratives within and across the periods they study. • Develop the appropriate use of historical terms. • Regularly address and sometimes devise historically valid questions about change, cause, similarity and difference, and significance.
3	• Can discuss the merits and faults of Julius Caesar. • Can describe the main events of Julius Caesar's invasions of Britain in 55BC and 54BC.	• Develop a chronologically secure knowledge and understanding of British, local and world history, establishing clear narratives within and across the periods they study. • Regularly address and sometimes devise historically valid questions about change, cause, similarity and difference, and significance.
4	• Can describe the main events of the Roman invasion of AD43. • Can describe how Caratacus resisted the Roman invaders.	• Develop a chronologically secure knowledge and understanding of British, local and world history, establishing clear narratives within and across the periods they study. • Regularly address and sometimes devise historically valid questions about change, cause, similarity and difference, and significance.
5	• Can describe where the Romans settled in Britain. • Can describe how written evidence has helped us to understand what Queen Boudica was like.	• Develop a chronologically secure knowledge and understanding of British, local and world history, establishing clear narratives within and across the periods they study. • Develop the appropriate use of historical terms. • Regularly address and sometimes devise historically valid questions about change, cause, similarity and difference, and significance.
6	• Can describe the main events of Boudica's rebellion. • Can identify why Celts and Romans may have differed in their opinions of Boudica.	• Develop a chronologically secure knowledge and understanding of British, local and world history, establishing clear narratives within and across the periods they study. • Understand how our knowledge of the past is constructed from a range of sources. • Understand that different versions of past events may exist, giving some reasons for this.
Assess and review		• To assess the half-term's work.

Medium-term planning Summer 2: Roman Britain (2)

National Curriculum objective
Children should be taught about: • the Roman Empire and its impact on Britain

W	Outcomes	Historical concepts
1	• Can describe the way that Roman Britain was organised. • Can describe life in a town in Roman Britain.	• Develop a chronologically secure knowledge and understanding of British, local and world history, establishing clear narratives within and across the periods they study. • Note connections, contrasts and trends over time and develop the appropriate use of historical terms. • Regularly address and sometimes devise historically valid questions about change, cause, similarity and difference, and significance.
2	• Can describe the construction of Roman roads in Britain. • Can describe the beginnings of early Christianity in Britain.	• (same as week 1)
3	• Can describe how life for the Celts changed under Roman rule. • Can understand how archaeological sites like Caerwent give us information about the Roman period.	• Develop a chronologically secure knowledge and understanding of British, local and world history, establishing clear narratives within and across the periods they study. • Note connections, contrasts and trends over time. • Regularly address and sometimes devise historically valid questions about change, cause, similarity and difference, and significance. • Understand how our knowledge of the past is constructed from a range of sources.
4	• Can describe why Hadrian's Wall was built. • Can describe what life might have been like for a soldier at a Hadrian's Wall fort.	• Develop a chronologically secure knowledge and understanding of British, local and world history, establishing clear narratives within and across the periods they study. • Note connections, contrasts and trends over time. • Regularly address and sometimes devise historically valid questions about change, cause, similarity and difference, and significance. • Understand how our knowledge of the past is constructed from a range of sources.
5	• Visit a Roman site in their local area (option to research a Roman site online if this isn't possible). • Can create a presentation about an aspect of Roman British life.	• Develop a chronologically secure knowledge and understanding of British, local and world history, establishing clear narratives within and across the periods they study. • Note connections, contrasts and trends over time. • Regularly address and sometimes devise historically valid questions about change, cause, similarity and difference, and significance. • Understand how our knowledge of the past is constructed from a range of sources. • Understand that different versions of past events may exist, giving some reasons for this.
6	• Can continue work on a presentation about an aspect of Roman British life. • Can present their own information about an aspect of Roman British life.	• Develop a chronologically secure knowledge and understanding of British, local and world history, establishing clear narratives within and across the periods they study. • Note connections, contrasts and trends over time. • Regularly address and sometimes devise historically valid questions about change, cause, similarity and difference, and significance. • Understand how our knowledge of the past is constructed from a range of sources.
Assess and review		• To assess the half-term's work.

Year 4 Background knowledge

Year 4 content begins with the wider world, with children exploring two of the most influential cultures – ancient Greece and the Roman Empire – before continuing the chronological narrative of British history. Children consolidate their knowledge of the Celts, developed in Year 3, as they consider the impact of the Roman invasion. While topics follow the chronological history of Britain and the wider world, core history skills should develop as children progress through the different topics and these have been woven into the content planning.

Understanding chronology and timelines

In Year 4, children develop their understanding of chronology, considering events and civilisations that existed in different areas of the world within the same time period (the Iron Age Celts in Britain running alongside the expansion of the Roman Empire). They build on their understanding from Year 3 of how different historical periods fit together (the history of Britain from the Stone Age through the Bronze and Iron Ages to the period of Roman rule from AD43). During the topics, children are given many opportunities to progress their skills in interpreting and constructing timelines to show when significant events occurred. They understand that these can cover short-term timescales (key events of Boudica's revolt against the Romans) or long-term timescales crossing from 'Before Christ' to 'Anno Domini'.

Addressing and devising historically valid questions

In every topic, children have many opportunities to address historically valid questions (What happened at the ancient Greek Olympic Games? How did ancient Greek theatre influence modern theatre? Who was Julius Caesar? How did life for the Celts change under Roman rule?) using a range of reliable sources to find answers. Particularly when using the internet, it is important that children understand the difference between a reliable and non-reliable source of information and between fact and opinion. At the end of the year, children are given the opportunity to devise their own historically valid questions and carry out an independent investigation into an area of personal interest on the topic of Roman Britain, sharing their findings through a project or presentation.

Constructing and interpreting the past from evidence

As children progress as historians, they view the past less in terms of facts and more as knowledge constructed from evidence. This evidence could be written (Cassius Dio's description of Boudica, the writings of Plato, Aesop's fables), from archaeological sites (the Acropolis, the Roman Forum, Hadrian's Wall) or artefacts (Greek pottery and sculptures, the Vindolanda tablets), or even from eyewitness reports (Pliny the Younger's account of the eruption of Vesuvius in AD79). The children also progress in their understanding that evidence of the past is interpreted in different ways and that historical people and events can be viewed differently (Boudica as a great queen who tried to free her people from Roman oppression or a brutal avenger who slaughtered Celts and Romans alike). They begin to use the evidence to construct their own interpretations.

Understanding cause, consequence and significance

In the different topics, children have opportunities to consider the cause and consequences of different events (such as the events leading up to the Roman invasion of Britain, its immediate impact and its legacy today). Children examine the reasons behind events as well as the events themselves. This gives a good starting point for understanding which events can be considered historically significant (the murder of Julius Caesar influencing the establishment of Augustus as the first Emperor of Rome).

Drawing comparisons

Throughout the scheme of work there are opportunities for children to make observations and draw comparisons. In Year 4, they consider the similarities and differences between past civilisations (the weaponry, armour and tactics of the Celt warriors as opposed to the Roman army; the contrasting role of women in Celt versus Roman society), as well as comparing life in the past with life today (a chariot race in ancient Rome compared with a modern-day football match; the ancient and modern Olympic Games).

Analysing change and trends over time

More able children may begin to develop the ability to analyse historical change and spot trends over time, a skill which they will further progress in Year 5 and beyond. As they add to the knowledge they acquired in Year 3, certain historical themes and patterns emerge (changes to the development of tools and weapons and the impact of new technology).

Year 5 Long-term planning

1. *Children should know and understand the history of these islands as a coherent, chronological narrative, from the earliest times to the present day: how people's lives have shaped this nation and how Britain has influenced and been influenced by the wider world.*
Within the Year 5 chapters, children continue to learn about the historical narrative of Britain's history, exploring it from the Roman withdrawal in AD410, through invasion and settlement by the Anglo-Saxons.

2. *Children should know and understand significant aspects of the history of the wider world: the nature of ancient civilisations; the expansion and dissolution of empires; characteristic features of past non-European societies; achievements and follies of mankind.*
Within the Year 5 chapters, children will study a non-European society that provides contrasts with British history – the Maya civilisation *circa* AD900. They will examine the characteristic features of Maya society and compare and contrast them with the features of Anglo-Saxon society in Britain at around the same time.

3. *Children should gain and deploy a historically grounded understanding of abstract terms such as 'empire', 'civilisation', 'parliament' and 'peasantry'.*
Within Year 5, children develop their understanding of a wide variety of such terms (for example, 'invasion', 'settlement', 'kingdom', 'culture', 'conversion', 'evidence' and 'significance').

4. *Children should understand historical concepts such as continuity and change, cause and consequence, similarity, difference and significance, and use them to make connections, draw contrasts, analyse trends, frame historically valid questions and create their own structured accounts, including written narratives and analyses.*
Within all six Year 5 chapters, children are given the opportunity to learn about the above historical concepts and use them in the ways described. In the final week of Chapter 4 children research, analyse and answer historically valid questions about the ancient Maya civilisation that they have devised themselves. The local history study in Chapters 5 and 6 is based entirely around historical questions framed by the children.

5. *Children should understand the methods of historical enquiry, including how evidence is used rigorously to make historical claims, and discern how and why contrasting arguments and interpretations of the past have been constructed.*
Within the Year 5 chapters, children are introduced to historical enquiry and interpretations of the past via written and archaeological evidence, as well as artefacts and eyewitness reports. They begin to examine evidence more critically and understand that this can be interpreted in a number of ways.

6. *Children should gain historical perspective by placing their growing knowledge into different contexts, understanding the connections between local, regional, national and international history; between cultural, economic, military, political, religious and social history; and between short- and long-term timescales.*
Within the Year 5 chapters, children explore the connections between national and international history, comparing the Maya with the Anglo-Saxons. They study both societies in terms of culture, art, architecture, military strategy, religion and mythology, social structure and government. They study an aspect of local history, making links, where possible, with topics already studied in national history. The Year 5 chapters encompass widely varying timescales – from events lasting a few weeks to the achievements of civilisations over hundreds of years; from events that happened within living memory to those that took place more than fifteen hundred years ago.

Overview of progression in Year 5

Children should continue to develop a chronologically secure knowledge and understanding of British, local and world history, establishing clear narratives within and across the periods they study. They should note connections, contrasts and trends over time and develop the appropriate use of historical terms. They should regularly address and sometimes devise historically valid questions about change, cause, similarity and difference, and significance. They should construct informed responses that involve thoughtful selection and organisation of relevant historical information. They should understand how our knowledge of the past is constructed from a range of sources.

In planning to ensure the progression described above through teaching the British, local and world history outlined below, teachers should combine overview and depth studies to help pupils understand both the long arc of development and the complexity of specific aspects of the content.

Children should be taught about:

- *Britain's settlement by Anglo-Saxons and Scots*

Children learn who the Anglo-Saxons and Scots were, and how and why they came to Britain. They investigate Anglo-Saxon culture including language, literature and religion, and they learn how the Anglo-Saxons were converted to Christianity. They consider which aspects of the Anglo-Saxons' legacy are most significant.

- *a non-European society that provides contrasts with British history: Mayan civilisation* circa AD900

Children explore ancient Maya architecture, social structure, law and order, games, stories, food, art, writing, trade, calendars, mathematics, science, and religion. They make comparisons between the Maya and the Anglo-Saxons, and investigate the mystery of why the ancient Maya civilisation collapsed.

- *a local history study*

Children decide which aspect of local history to investigate, and which questions they want to answer. They gather evidence from a wide range of sources, and use it to form their own historical theories. Finally, they share these theories with a wider audience, using a method of their choice.

Overview and depth studies

The planning incorporates both overview studies and depth studies, but you may choose to adapt lessons to focus on certain topics in more detail or to skip lessons to shorten topics.

Depth studies could include the following:

Autumn 1: the excavations at Sutton Hoo and what they reveal about Anglo-Saxon life and culture

Autumn 2: Anglo-Saxon literature: myths, legends and poetry

Spring 1: a study of one of the major ancient Maya cities, such as Palenque, Tikal or Caracol

Spring 2: an investigation into the part played by agriculture in ancient Maya civilisation, including the central role of maize in not only diet, but also culture and religion

Summer 1 & 2: the local history study could be a depth study linked to one of the areas of British history already covered in Key Stage 2 (Britain from the Stone Age to the Iron Age, or Britain in Roman or Anglo-Saxon times)

Note: the outcomes, objectives and concepts outlined in the medium-term planning grids for each week are spread across two lessons

Medium-term planning Autumn 1: The Anglo-Saxons (1)

National Curriculum objective

Children should be taught about:
• Britain's settlement by Anglo-Saxons and Scots

W	Outcomes	Historical concepts
1	• Can explain why the Romans abandoned Britain. • Can describe how and why the Scots and Anglo-Saxons came to Britain and can discuss whether they should be described as invaders or settlers.	• Develop a chronologically secure knowledge and understanding of British, local and world history, establishing clear narratives within and across the periods they study. • Develop the appropriate use of historical terms. • Regularly address and sometimes devise historically valid questions about change, cause, similarity and difference, and significance.
2	• Can describe the appearance of Anglo-Saxon men, women and children at various levels of society. • Can draw comparisons between Anglo-Saxon weaponry and armour and those of the Romans. The children can use these comparisons to make a value judgment about fighting effectiveness.	• Develop a chronologically secure knowledge and understanding of British, local and world history, establishing clear narratives within and across the periods they study. • Note connections, contrasts and trends over time. • Regularly address and sometimes devise historically valid questions about change, cause, similarity and difference, and significance.
3	• Can identify the main areas of Britain where the Anglo-Saxons settled. • Can identify some place names of Anglo-Saxon origin, explain what some of them mean, and discuss what these meanings tell us about Anglo-Saxon life.	• Develop a chronologically secure knowledge and understanding of British, local and world history, establishing clear narratives within and across the periods they study. • Note connections, contrasts and trends over time. • Understand how our knowledge of the past is constructed from a range of sources.
4	• Can describe in general terms how Britain was ruled in Anglo-Saxon times. • Can describe some laws in Anglo-Saxon Britain and express their judgement about whether those laws were fair.	• Develop a chronologically secure knowledge and understanding of British, local and world history, establishing clear narratives within and across the periods they study. • Develop the appropriate use of historical terms. • Construct informed responses that involve thoughtful selection and organisation of relevant historical information.
5	• Can describe a typical home in Anglo-Saxon Britain. • Can draw comparisons between Anglo-Saxon villages and Roman towns, explaining which they would rather live in, and why.	• Develop a chronologically secure knowledge and understanding of British, local and world history, establishing clear narratives within and across the periods they study. • Note connections, contrasts and trends over time and develop the appropriate use of historical terms. • Regularly address and sometimes devise historically valid questions about change, cause, similarity and difference, and significance.
6	• Can identify and classify some of the sources of evidence we have for what life was like in Anglo-Saxon Britain, and can suggest what these sources tell us. • Can explain what the Sutton Hoo ship burial tells us about the person buried there and about life in Anglo-Saxon Britain.	• Develop a chronologically secure knowledge and understanding of British, local and world history, establishing clear narratives within and across the periods they study. • Develop the appropriate use of historical terms. • Understand how our knowledge of the past is constructed from a range of sources.
Assess and review		• To assess the half-term's work.

Medium-term planning Autumn 2: The Anglo-Saxons (2)

National Curriculum objective

Children should be taught about:
- Britain's settlement by Anglo-Saxons and Scots

W	Outcomes	Historical concepts
1	• Can identify differences between daily life in Anglo-Saxon times and daily life today; can express and justify their opinions about these differences. • Can describe some important features of Anglo-Saxon childhood and distinguish between the lives of boys and girls.	• Develop a chronologically secure knowledge and understanding of British, local and world history, establishing clear narratives within and across the periods they study. • Note connections, contrasts and trends over time. • Regularly address and sometimes devise historically valid questions about change, cause, similarity and difference, and significance.
2	• Can describe Anglo-Saxon food and express their opinions about it. • Can create an original design in an Anglo-Saxon style.	• Develop a chronologically secure knowledge and understanding of British, local and world history, establishing clear narratives within and across the periods they study.
3	• Can name some modern English words of Anglo-Saxon origin and compare their present day form with their original form. • Can write their names in Anglo-Saxon runes.	• Develop a chronologically secure knowledge and understanding of British, local and world history, establishing clear narratives within and across the periods they study. • Note connections, contrasts and trends over time. • Regularly address and sometimes devise historically valid questions about change, cause, similarity and difference, and significance.
4	• Can retell part of the legend of Beowulf and discuss what the story tells us about the Anglo-Saxons. • Can name the principle gods and goddesses worshipped by the Anglo-Saxons. • Can explain the link between Anglo-Saxon gods and the modern days of the week.	• Develop a chronologically secure knowledge and understanding of British, local and world history, establishing clear narratives within and across the periods they study. • Regularly address and sometimes devise historically valid questions about change, cause, similarity and difference, and significance. • Note connections, contrasts and trends over time. • Understand how our knowledge of the past is constructed from a range of sources.
5	• Can describe how the Anglo-Saxons were converted to Christianity. • Can explain the significance of the Lindisfarne Gospels.	• Develop a chronologically secure knowledge and understanding of British, local and world history, establishing clear narratives within and across the periods they study. • Develop the appropriate use of historical terms. • Regularly address and sometimes devise historically valid questions about change, cause, similarity and difference, and significance.
6	• Can create a timeline of Anglo-Saxon Britain. • Can debate the importance of various aspects of the Anglo-Saxons' legacy.	• Develop a chronologically secure knowledge and understanding of British, local and world history, establishing clear narratives within and across the periods they study. • Note connections, contrasts and trends over time and develop the appropriate use of historical terms. • Regularly address and sometimes devise historically valid questions about change, cause, similarity and difference, and significance. • Construct informed responses that involve thoughtful selection and organisation of relevant historical information.
Assess and review		• To assess the half-term's work.

Medium-term planning Spring 1: The Maya (1)

National Curriculum objective

Children should be taught about:

• a non-European society that provides contrasts with British history – one study chosen from: early Islamic civilisation, including a study of Baghdad *circa* AD900; Mayan civilisation *circa* AD900; Benin (West Africa) *circa* AD900-1300

W	Outcomes	Historical concepts
1	• Can locate the ancient Maya civilisation on a map of the world and on a timeline. • Can describe some of the evidence left behind by the ancient Maya civilisation.	• Develop a chronologically secure knowledge and understanding of British, local and world history, establishing clear narratives within and across the periods they study. • Understand how our knowledge of the past is constructed from a range of sources.
2	• Can explain what the palace at Palenque tells us about the ancient Maya civilisation. • Can draw comparisons between the Maya pyramids and the pyramids of Ancient Egypt.	• Develop a chronologically secure knowledge and understanding of British, local and world history, establishing clear narratives within and across the periods they study. • Construct informed responses that involve thoughtful selection and organisation of relevant historical information. • Understand how our knowledge of the past is constructed from a range of sources.
3	• Can explain what stelae are and can explain some of the things they tell us about the ancient Maya. • Can design authentic-looking Maya costumes.	• Develop a chronologically secure knowledge and understanding of British, local and world history, establishing clear narratives within and across the periods they study. • Develop the appropriate use of historical terms. • Understand how our knowledge of the past is constructed from a range of sources.
4	• Can draw comparisons between ancient Maya homes and Anglo-Saxon homes. They can express and justify their preferences. • Can draw comparisons between Chichen Itza and ancient Rome. Children can suggest what an ancient Roman might have thought of Chichen Itza.	• Develop a chronologically secure knowledge and understanding of British, local and world history, establishing clear narratives within and across the periods they study. • Note connections, contrasts and trends over time. • Regularly address and sometimes devise historically valid questions about change, cause, similarity and difference, and significance.
5	• Can describe how the Maya were ruled. • Can describe some ancient Maya laws, and compare and contrast them with laws in Anglo-Saxon Britain.	• Develop a chronologically secure knowledge and understanding of British, local and world history, establishing clear narratives within and across the periods they study. • Note connections, contrasts and trends over time. • Regularly address and sometimes devise historically valid questions about change, cause, similarity and difference, and significance.
6	• Can describe the ballgame played by the Maya, and devise and play a similar ballgame. • Can retell the Maya creation myth.	• Develop a chronologically secure knowledge and understanding of British, local and world history, establishing clear narratives within and across the periods they study.
Assess and review		• To assess the half-term's work.

Medium-term planning Spring 2: The Maya (2)

National Curriculum objective

Children should be taught about:
- a non-European society that provides contrasts with British history – one study chosen from: early Islamic civilisation, including a study of Baghdad *circa* AD900; Mayan civilisation *circa* AD900; Benin (West Africa) *circa* AD900-1300

W	Outcomes	Historical concepts
1	• Can describe the diet of the ancient Maya. • Can compare the art of the ancient Maya with the art of the Anglo-Saxons.	• Develop a chronologically secure knowledge and understanding of British, local and world history, establishing clear narratives within and across the periods they study. • Note connections, contrasts and trends over time. • Regularly address and sometimes devise historically valid questions about change, cause, similarity and difference, and significance.
2	• Can recognise Maya glyphs and use syllable glyphs to write their names. • Can name some of the goods the ancient Maya traded with their neighbours. • Can explain the impact of this trade on the ancient Maya civilisation.	• Develop a chronologically secure knowledge and understanding of British, local and world history, establishing clear narratives within and across the periods they study. • Regularly address and sometimes devise historically valid questions about change, cause, similarity and difference, and significance.
3	• Children can give a simple explanation of how the ancient Maya calendar worked. • Can describe some of the Maya's scientific and mathematical achievements. • Can read and write numbers in the Maya number system.	• Develop a chronologically secure knowledge and understanding of British, local and world history, establishing clear narratives within and across the periods they study.
4	• Can describe some ancient Maya religious beliefs and practices. • Can evaluate how important religion was to the ancient Maya. • Can compare the burial rites of the ancient Maya to those of the Anglo-Saxons.	• Develop a chronologically secure knowledge and understanding of British, local and world history, establishing clear narratives within and across the periods they study. • Note connections, contrasts and trends over time. • Regularly address and sometimes devise historically valid questions about change, cause, similarity and difference, and significance.
5	• Can discuss the comparative levels of civilisation of the ancient Maya and the Anglo-Saxons. • Can evaluate the evidence in support of several theories about the causes of the collapse of the ancient Maya civilisation. • Can say which theory they think is most convincing, and explain why.	• Develop a chronologically secure knowledge and understanding of British, local and world history, establishing clear narratives within and across the periods they study. • Develop the appropriate use of historical terms. • Regularly address and sometimes devise historically valid questions about change, cause, similarity and difference, and significance. • Construct informed responses that involve thoughtful selection and organisation of relevant historical information. • Understand how our knowledge of the past is constructed from a range of sources.
6	• Can devise historically valid questions about the ancient Maya civilisation and research answers to their questions, evaluating the sources they use for reliability. • Can choose an appropriate method of presenting what they have found out. • Can prepare and give a presentation of their findings.	• Develop a chronologically secure knowledge and understanding of British, local and world history, establishing clear narratives within and across the periods they study. • Regularly address and sometimes devise historically valid questions about change, cause, similarity and difference, and significance. • Construct informed responses that involve thoughtful selection and organisation of relevant historical information.
Assess and review		• To assess the half-term's work.

YEAR 5

National Curriculum objective

Children should be taught about:
• a local history study

W	Outcomes	Historical concepts
1	• Can decide which aspect of local history to study from a range of choices. • Can decide how they will share what they find out during the study and who they will share it with.	• Develop a chronologically secure knowledge and understanding of British, local and world history, establishing clear narratives within and across the periods they study.
2	• Can frame historically relevant questions about the aspect of local history they have chosen to study. • Can identify a range of sources they could use to find out the answers to their questions.	• Develop a chronologically secure knowledge and understanding of British, local and world history, establishing clear narratives within and across the periods they study. • Regularly address and sometimes devise historically valid questions about change, cause, similarity and difference, and significance. • Understand how our knowledge of the past is constructed from a range of sources.
3	• Can evaluate evidence from a range of sources. • Can use interviews and/or surveys to gather historical evidence.	• Develop a chronologically secure knowledge and understanding of British, local and world history, establishing clear narratives within and across the periods they study. • Regularly address and sometimes devise historically valid questions about change, cause, similarity and difference, and significance. • Construct informed responses that involve thoughtful selection and organisation of relevant historical information. • Understand how our knowledge of the past is constructed from a range of sources.
4	• Can use buildings to gather historical evidence. • Can use a visit to an archaeological site to gather historical evidence.	• Develop a chronologically secure knowledge and understanding of British, local and world history, establishing clear narratives within and across the periods they study. • Understand how our knowledge of the past is constructed from a range of sources.
5	• Can use artefacts to gather historical evidence. • Can use gravestones to gather historical evidence.	• Develop a chronologically secure knowledge and understanding of British, local and world history, establishing clear narratives within and across the periods they study. • Understand how our knowledge of the past is constructed from a range of sources.
6	• Can use a visit to a local museum to gather historical evidence. • Can use a visit by a local historian to gather historical evidence.	• Develop a chronologically secure knowledge and understanding of British, local and world history, establishing clear narratives within and across the periods they study. • Understand how our knowledge of the past is constructed from a range of sources.
Assess and review		• To assess the half-term's work.

Medium-term planning Summer 2: A local history study (2)

National Curriculum objective

Children should be taught about:
- a local history study

W	Outcomes	Historical concepts
1	• Can use old newspapers to gather historical evidence. • Can use old maps to gather historical evidence.	• Develop a chronologically secure knowledge and understanding of British, local and world history, establishing clear narratives within and across the periods they study. • Understand how our knowledge of the past is constructed from a range of sources.
2	• Can use old photographs to gather historical evidence. • Can use public records to gather historical evidence.	• Develop a chronologically secure knowledge and understanding of British, local and world history, establishing clear narratives within and across the periods they study. • Understand how our knowledge of the past is constructed from a range of sources.
3	• Can use old school logbooks to gather historical evidence. • Can use personal documents to gather historical evidence.	• Develop a chronologically secure knowledge and understanding of British, local and world history, establishing clear narratives within and across the periods they study. • Understand how our knowledge of the past is constructed from a range of sources.
4	• Can use books on local history to gather historical evidence. • Can make connections between their locality's past and present.	• Develop a chronologically secure knowledge and understanding of British, local and world history, establishing clear narratives within and across the periods they study. • Note connections, contrasts and trends over time. • Understand how our knowledge of the past is constructed from a range of sources.
5	• Can make connections between local history and British history. • Can prepare a presentation on local history.	• Develop a chronologically secure knowledge and understanding of British, local and world history, establishing clear narratives within and across the periods they study. • Note connections, contrasts and trends over time. • Construct informed responses that involve thoughtful selection and organisation of relevant historical information.
6	• Can present the results of their local history study. • Can evaluate their learning.	• Develop a chronologically secure knowledge and understanding of British, local and world history, establishing clear narratives within and across the periods they study.
Assess and review		• To assess the half-term's work.

Year 5 Background knowledge

The Year 5 content begins by continuing the chronological narrative of British history. Children consolidate their knowledge of the Romans, developed in Year 4, by considering the impact of the Roman withdrawal from Britain and of the subsequent invasion and settlement of Britain by Scots and Anglo-Saxons. The focus moves to exploring a contrasting non-European culture of around the same time – the ancient Maya civilisation. In the summer term the focus returns to Britain with a local history study. There are opportunities to link this study to an area of British history already covered in Key Stage 2, or to use it to extend the children's knowledge of an aspect of British history beyond ancient times, into the middle ages and the modern era. While topics follow the chronological history of Britain and the wider world, core history skills will develop as children progress through the different topics.

Understanding chronology and timelines

In Year 5, children develop their understanding of chronology, considering events and civilisations that existed in different areas of the world within the same time period (the Anglo-Saxons in Britain running alongside the ancient Maya civilisation in Mesoamerica). They build on their understanding from Year 4 of how different historical periods fit together (the period of Roman rule from AD43 to the first Viking raids in AD793). During the topics, children are given many opportunities to progress their skills in interpreting and constructing timelines to show when significant events occurred. They understand that these can cover short-term timescales (such as key events in the Anglo-Saxon invasion of Britain) or long-term timescales of over a thousand years (such as looking at changes in an aspect of local history from Anglo-Saxon times to the present day).

Addressing and devising historically valid questions

In every topic, children have many opportunities to address historically valid questions (why did the Romans leave Britain? How did Anglo-Saxon settlements compare to Roman towns? What evidence have the Maya people left behind? How did trade affect the way the Maya people lived?) using a range of reliable sources to find answers. Particularly when using the internet, it is important that children understand the difference between a reliable and non-reliable source of information and between fact and opinion. In the local history study in the summer term, children are given the opportunity to devise their own historically valid questions and carry out an independent investigation into an area of personal interest on the topic of local history, sharing their findings through a project or presentation.

Constructing and interpreting the past from evidence

As children progress as historians, they view the past less in terms of facts and more as knowledge constructed from evidence. This evidence could be written (Lindisfarne Gospels), from archaeological sites (Sutton Hoo) or artefacts (Maya *stelae*), or even from eyewitness reports. In Year 5, children also progress in their understanding that evidence of the past is interpreted in different ways and that historical people and events can be viewed differently. Children begin to use the evidence to construct their own interpretations.

Understanding cause, consequence and significance

In the different topics, children have opportunities to consider the cause and consequences of different events (such as the events leading up to the Roman withdrawal from Britain, and its immediate and longer-term impact). Children examine the reasons behind events as well as the events themselves. This gives a good starting point for understanding which events can be considered historically significant (an event in local history precipitating, affecting or being affected by an event happening on a national scale).

Drawing comparisons

Throughout this scheme of work there are opportunities for children to make observations and draw comparisons. In Year 5, they consider the similarities and differences between past civilisations (the Maya pyramids as opposed to the pyramids of ancient Egypt) as well as comparing life in the past with life today (daily life in Anglo-Saxon times compared with daily life today).

Analysing change and trends over time

In Year 5, more able children may begin to develop the ability to analyse historical change and spot trends over time, a skill which they will further progress in Year 6. As their knowledge base grows and they add to the knowledge they acquired in Year 4, certain historical themes and patterns emerge.

Year 6 Long-term planning

1. *Children should know and understand the history of these islands as a coherent, chronological narrative, from the earliest times to the present day: how people's lives have shaped this nation and how Britain has influenced and been influenced by the wider world.*
   Within the Year 6 chapters, children will continue to learn about the historical narrative of Britain's history, exploring it from the first Viking invasions in the late 8th century to the death of Edward the Confessor in 1066. The Year 6 chapters also include studies that extend children's chronological knowledge of Britain beyond 1066: a study of medicine from Anglo-Saxon times to the present day and a study of the Battle of Britain; a significant turning point in British history.

2. *Children should know and understand significant aspects of the history of the wider world: the nature of ancient civilisations; the expansion and dissolution of empires; characteristic features of past non-European societies; achievements and follies of mankind.*
   Within the Year 6 chapters, children will study a non-European society that provides contrasts with British history – early Islamic civilisation, including a study of Baghdad circa AD900. They will examine the characteristic features of early Islamic society and compare and contrast them with the features of Viking society in Britain at around the same time.

3. *Children should gain and deploy a historically grounded understanding of abstract terms such as 'empire', 'civilisation', 'parliament' and 'peasantry'.*
   Within Year 6, children develop their understanding of a wide variety of such terms (for example: 'reliability', 'justification', 'theory', 'factors', 'impact', 'context' and 'strategy').

4. *Children should understand historical concepts such as continuity and change, cause and consequence, similarity, difference and significance, and use them to make connections, draw contrasts, analyse trends, frame historically valid questions and create their own structured accounts, including written narratives and analyses.*
   Within all six Year 6 chapters, children are given the opportunity to learn about the above historical concepts and to use them in the ways described. In the final week of chapters 4 and 6, children research, analyse and answer historically valid questions that they have devised themselves about the history of medicine and about early Islamic civilisation.

5. *Children should understand the methods of historical enquiry, including how evidence is used rigorously to make historical claims, and discern how and why contrasting arguments and interpretations of the past have been constructed.*
   Within the Year 6 chapters, children are introduced to historical enquiry and interpretations of the past via written and archaeological evidence, as well as artefacts and eyewitness reports. They examine evidence critically and understand that it can be interpreted in a number of ways.

6. *Children should gain historical perspective by placing their growing knowledge into different contexts, understanding the connections between local, regional, national and international history; between cultural, economic, military, political, religious and social history; and between short- and long-term timescales.*
   Within the Year 6 chapters, children explore the connections between national and international history, comparing early Islamic civilisation with Viking Britain. They study both societies in terms of culture, art, architecture, religion, social structure and government. The Year 6 chapters encompass widely varying timescales – from events lasting a few weeks to the achievements of civilisations over hundreds of years; from events that happened within living memory to those that took place more than fifteen hundred years ago.

Overview of progression in Year 6

Children should continue to develop a chronologically secure knowledge and understanding of British, local and world history, establishing clear narratives within and across the periods they study. They should note connections, contrasts and trends over time and develop the appropriate use of historical terms. They should regularly address and sometimes devise historically valid questions about change, cause, similarity and difference, and significance. They should construct informed responses that involve thoughtful selection and organisation of relevant historical information. They should understand how our knowledge of the past is constructed from a range of sources.

In planning to ensure the progression described above through teaching the British, local and world history outlined below, teachers should combine overview and depth studies to help pupils understand both the long arc of development and the complexity of specific aspects of the content.

Children should be taught about:

- *the Viking and Anglo-Saxon struggle for the Kingdom of England to the time of Edward the Confessor*

Children learn about Viking culture, and look at the part played by Alfred the Great, Athelstan, Ethelred and Canute in the struggle for control of England.

- *a study of an aspect or theme in British history that extends pupils' chronological knowledge beyond 1066*

  - *changes in an aspect of social history: medicine from the Anglo-Saxons to the present*

Children investigate advances in medicine since Anglo-Saxon times, and the huge impact they have had on everyday life in Britain.

  - *a significant turning point in British history: The Battle of Britain*

Children learn about the people and events of the Battle of Britain, and why it was a major turning point in the nation's history. (This study could replace all or part of the study of the history of medicine in the spring term, be studied in addition to it, or be omitted altogether.)

- *a non-European society that provides contrasts with British history: early Islamic civilisation, including a study of Baghdad circa AD900*

Children study early Islamic social structure, art, and architecture. They compare daily life and religious beliefs with those of the Vikings. They examine the role of writing and learning, and consider the civilisation's contributions to science and mathematics. (This study could replace all or part of the study of the ancient Maya civilisation in the spring term of Year 5, be studied in addition to it, or be omitted altogether.)

Overview and depth studies

The planning incorporates both overview studies and depth studies, but you may choose to adapt lessons to focus on certain topics in more detail or to skip lessons to shorten topics.

Depth studies could include the following:

Autumn 1: Viking warfare: a study of Viking weapons, armour and military tactics

Autumn 2: how Viking sagas developed over time and in different parts of the Viking world

Spring 1: a study of the causes and effects of either the Black Death (1348–1350) or the Great Plague of London (1665–1666)

Spring 2: an investigation into how smallpox was eventually eradicated

Summer 1: the story of one of the Battle of Britain pilots, such as Douglas Bader

Summer 2: the life and work of one of the early Islamic scholars, such as Muhammad ibn Mūsā al-Khwārizmī

Note: the outcomes, objectives and concepts outlined in the medium-term planning grids for each week are spread across two lessons

■ SCHOLASTIC

Medium-term planning Autumn 1: The Vikings (1)

National Curriculum objective

Children should be taught about:
- the Viking and Anglo-Saxon struggle for the Kingdom of England to the time of Edward the Confessor

W	Outcomes	Historical concepts
1	• Can describe what they already know about the Vikings. • Can identify some of the sources of their knowledge and evaluate how accurate and reliable each source is likely to be. • Can explain who the Vikings were, where they came from, and how they got the name 'Vikings'.	• Develop a chronologically secure knowledge and understanding of British, local and world history, establishing clear narratives within and across the periods they study. • Understand how our knowledge of the past is constructed from a range of sources.
2	• Can evaluate the evidence for and against Viking helmets having horns. • Can describe the dress of a Viking warrior. • Can describe the weapons, armour and battle tactics of Viking warriors, and suggest why they were so feared.	• Develop a chronologically secure knowledge and understanding of British, local and world history, establishing clear narratives within and across the periods they study. • Construct informed responses that involve thoughtful selection and organisation of relevant historical information. • Regularly address and sometimes devise historically valid questions about change, cause, similarity and difference, and significance. • Understand how our knowledge of the past is constructed from a range of sources.
3	• Can describe the Viking attacks in general terms and identify when and where some of them took place. • Can describe Viking longships and can identify aspects of their design that contributed to the Vikings' success in raids.	• Develop a chronologically secure knowledge and understanding of British, local and world history, establishing clear narratives within and across the periods they study. • Regularly address and sometimes devise historically valid questions about change, cause, similarity and difference, and significance.
4	• Can explain some of the reasons why the Vikings came to Britain. • Can describe some of the archaeological evidence the Vikings left behind and explain what it tells us about Viking life.	• Develop a chronologically secure knowledge and understanding of British, local and world history, establishing clear narratives within and across the periods they study. • Develop the appropriate use of historical terms. • Regularly address and sometimes devise historically valid questions about change, cause, similarity and difference, and significance. • Understand how our knowledge of the past is constructed from a range of sources.
5	• Can describe some of the written sources we have for our knowledge about the Vikings and can explain what they tell us. • Can say whether they think women were treated fairly in Viking society, and can use evidence to support their argument.	• Develop a chronologically secure knowledge and understanding of British, local and world history, establishing clear narratives within and across the periods they study. • Understand how our knowledge of the past is constructed from a range of sources. • Construct informed responses that involve thoughtful selection and organisation of relevant historical information.
6	• Can describe the features of a Viking longhouse. • Can describe some of the main features of daily life in a Viking village, say whether they would want to live in one, and explain why.	• Develop a chronologically secure knowledge and understanding of British, local and world history, establishing clear narratives within and across the periods they study. • Construct informed responses that involve thoughtful selection and organisation of relevant historical information.
Assess and review		• To assess the half-term's work.

Medium-term planning Autumn 2: The Vikings (2)

National Curriculum objective

Children should be taught about:
• the Viking and Anglo-Saxon struggle for the Kingdom of England to the time of Edward the Confessor

W	Outcomes	Historical concepts
1	• Can describe the Viking diet and say whether or not they would like to eat Viking food. • Can draw comparisons between Viking and Anglo-Saxon art and suggest possible reasons for the similarities.	• Develop a chronologically secure knowledge and understanding of British, local and world history, establishing clear narratives within and across the periods they study. • Regularly address and sometimes devise historically valid questions about change, cause, similarity and difference, and significance.
2	• Can identify similarities between the Viking and Anglo-Saxon gods, and suggest possible reasons for them. • Can explain the role of sagas in Viking culture, and can retell the story of a least one saga.	• Develop a chronologically secure knowledge and understanding of British, local and world history, establishing clear narratives within and across the periods they study. • Regularly address and sometimes devise historically valid questions about change, cause, similarity and difference, and significance.
3	• Can draw comparisons between Viking burial practices and those of the ancient Maya. • Can explain who King Alfred was, the part he played in British history, and why he was given the title 'the Great'.	• Develop a chronologically secure knowledge and understanding of British, local and world history, establishing clear narratives within and across the periods they study. • Note connections, contrasts and trends over time. • Regularly address and sometimes devise historically valid questions about change, cause, similarity and difference, and significance.
4	• Can explain the meaning of the term 'Danelaw'. • Can identify the areas of the country covered by the Danelaw. • Can explain who Athelstan was and why he is an important figure in British history.	• Develop a chronologically secure knowledge and understanding of British, local and world history, establishing clear narratives within and across the periods they study. • Regularly address and sometimes devise historically valid questions about change, cause, similarity and difference, and significance.
5	• Can explain what the Danegeld was. • Can express and justify their opinion about whether Ethelred should have paid the Danegeld. • Can explain the significance of King Canute in the history of Britain.	• Develop a chronologically secure knowledge and understanding of British, local and world history, establishing clear narratives within and across the periods they study. • Develop the appropriate use of historical terms. • Regularly address and sometimes devise historically valid questions about change, cause, similarity and difference, and significance. • Construct informed responses that involve thoughtful selection and organisation of relevant historical information.
6	• Can explain what happened to the Vikings. • Can create a timeline of Viking Age Britain.	• Develop a chronologically secure knowledge and understanding of British, local and world history, establishing clear narratives within and across the periods they study. • Note connections, contrasts and trends over time and develop the appropriate use of historical terms. • Develop the appropriate use of historical terms. • Regularly address and sometimes devise historically valid questions about change, cause, similarity and difference, and significance.
Assess and review		• To assess the half-term's work.

Medium-term planning Spring 1: Medicine (1)

National Curriculum objective

Children should be taught about:
- a study of an aspect or theme in British history that extends pupils' chronological knowledge beyond 1066

W	Outcomes	Historical concepts
1	• Can describe some early theories of disease. • Can describe some early medical treatments and explain why they were dangerous.	• Develop a chronologically secure knowledge and understanding of British, local and world history, establishing clear narratives within and across the periods they study. • Regularly address and sometimes devise historically valid questions about change, cause, similarity and difference, and significance.
2	• Can draw comparisons between the earliest hospitals in Britain and modern day hospitals. • Can identify some of the ways in which medical equipment has changed since Anglo-Saxon times.	• Develop a chronologically secure knowledge and understanding of British, local and world history, establishing clear narratives within and across the periods they study. • Note connections, contrasts and trends over time. • Regularly address and sometimes devise historically valid questions about change, cause, similarity and difference, and significance.
3	• Can describe some of the changes in dental care over the centuries. • Can describe some of the ways in which mental illness was treated in the past.	• Develop a chronologically secure knowledge and understanding of British, local and world history, establishing clear narratives within and across the periods they study. • Note connections, contrasts and trends over time. • Regularly address and sometimes devise historically valid questions about change, cause, similarity and difference, and significance.
4	• Can explain the main factors behind the rapid spread and high mortality rate of the plague. • Can describe the symptoms and causes of scurvy, and explain why it was once such a problem for sailors on long ocean voyages.	• Develop a chronologically secure knowledge and understanding of British, local and world history, establishing clear narratives within and across the periods they study. • Note connections, contrasts and trends over time. • Regularly address and sometimes devise historically valid questions about change, cause, similarity and difference, and significance. • Construct informed responses that involve thoughtful selection and organisation of relevant historical information.
5	• Can explain why smallpox was such a feared disease. • Can describe the part Edward Jenner played in the fight against smallpox.	• Develop a chronologically secure knowledge and understanding of British, local and world history, establishing clear narratives within and across the periods they study. • Regularly address and sometimes devise historically valid questions about change, cause, similarity and difference, and significance.
6	• Can describe various roles of women in the history of medicine and the way in which those roles have changed over the centuries. • Can describe the contribution Florence Nightingale made to medicine.	• Develop a chronologically secure knowledge and understanding of British, local and world history, establishing clear narratives within and across the periods they study. • Note connections, contrasts and trends over time. • Regularly address and sometimes devise historically valid questions about change, cause, similarity and difference, and significance.
Assess and review		• To assess the half-term's work.

Medium-term planning Spring 2: Medicine (2)

National Curriculum objective

Children should be taught about:
• a study of an aspect or theme in British history that extends pupils' chronological knowledge beyond 1066

W	Outcomes	Historical concepts
1	• Can describe the germ theory of disease and explain the impact it had on medical practices. • Can describe the major contributing factors to cholera outbreaks in Britain in the 19th century.	• Develop a chronologically secure knowledge and understanding of British, local and world history, establishing clear narratives within and across the periods they study. • Regularly address and sometimes devise historically valid questions about change, cause, similarity and difference, and significance.
2	• Can describe the contribution made by Edwin Chadwick to the development of medicine. • Can describe some of the advances in surgical techniques over the centuries, and can compare and contrast early surgery with modern surgery.	• Develop a chronologically secure knowledge and understanding of British, local and world history, establishing clear narratives within and across the periods they study. • Note connections, contrasts and trends over time. • Develop the appropriate use of historical terms. • Regularly address and sometimes devise historically valid questions about change, cause, similarity and difference, and significance.
3	• Can order anaesthetic developments on a timeline and explain the advantages associated with each new development. • Can explain the impact of Joseph Lister's pioneering work in antiseptic surgery.	• Develop a chronologically secure knowledge and understanding of British, local and world history, establishing clear narratives within and across the periods they study. • Note connections, contrasts and trends over time. • Regularly address and sometimes devise historically valid questions about change, cause, similarity and difference, and significance.
4	• Can describe the historical development of medical imaging technologies, including X-rays, magnetic resonance imaging and ultrasound. • Can explain some of the short- and long-term social effects of the flu pandemic 1918–1919.	• Develop a chronologically secure knowledge and understanding of British, local and world history, establishing clear narratives within and across the periods they study. • Note connections, contrasts and trends over time. • Regularly address and sometimes devise historically valid questions about change, cause, similarity and difference, and significance.
5	• Can relate the story of Alexander Fleming's discovery of penicillin and explain its significance. • Can describe the historical background of polio, and explain why babies are vaccinated against it.	• Develop a chronologically secure knowledge and understanding of British, local and world history, establishing clear narratives within and across the periods they study. • Regularly address and sometimes devise historically valid questions about change, cause, similarity and difference, and significance.
6	• Can explain the historical background to the setting up of the National Health Service in 1948, and explain the reasons behind it. • Can devise historically valid questions about the history of medicine. • Can research answers to their questions, evaluating the sources they use for reliability.	• Develop a chronologically secure knowledge and understanding of British, local and world history, establishing clear narratives within and across the periods they study. • Regularly address and sometimes devise historically valid questions about change, cause, similarity and difference, and significance. • Construct informed responses that involve thoughtful selection and organisation of relevant historical information. • Understand how our knowledge of the past is constructed from a range of sources.
Assess and review		• To assess the half-term's work.

Medium-term planning Summer 1: The Battle of Britain

National Curriculum objective

Children should be taught about:
- a study of an aspect or theme in British history that extends pupils' chronological knowledge beyond 1066

W	Outcomes	Historical concepts
1	• Can give a general description of the Battle of Britain, and show where it fits on a timeline. • Can identify some of the main sources of evidence we have for the Battle of Britain, and explain what each source tells us about the battle.	• Develop a chronologically secure knowledge and understanding of British, local and world history, establishing clear narratives within and across the periods they study. • Understand how our knowledge of the past is constructed from a range of sources.
2	• Can put the Battle of Britain within the wider context of World War II, and can describe the most significant events leading up to the battle. • Can name and describe the roles of the Allied and German leaders most directly involved in the Battle of Britain.	• Develop a chronologically secure knowledge and understanding of British, local and world history, establishing clear narratives within and across the periods they study. • Regularly address and sometimes devise historically valid questions about change, cause, similarity and difference, and significance.
3	• Can explain the significance of Churchill's famous quotation, explaining why 'so many' owe 'so much' to 'so few'. • Can describe and order the main events of the Battle of Britain.	• Develop a chronologically secure knowledge and understanding of British, local and world history, establishing clear narratives within and across the periods they study. • Regularly address and sometimes devise historically valid questions about change, cause, similarity and difference, and significance.
4	• Can identify and compare the principle aircraft in the Battle of Britain. • Can explain the strategy behind the bombing of London and other British cities, and evaluate whether or not it was successful.	• Develop a chronologically secure knowledge and understanding of British, local and world history, establishing clear narratives within and across the periods they study. • Regularly address and sometimes devise historically valid questions about change, cause, similarity and difference, and significance.
5	• Can identify some of the roles played by people on the ground in the Battle of Britain (radar operators, ARP wardens, rescue services, intelligence operatives, and so on). • Can describe what life was like in air raid shelters.	• Develop a chronologically secure knowledge and understanding of British, local and world history, establishing clear narratives within and across the periods they study.
6	• Can explain how the Battle of Britain ended. • Can evaluate the significance of the Battle of Britain within the wider context of World War II.	• Develop a chronologically secure knowledge and understanding of British, local and world history, establishing clear narratives within and across the periods they study. • Develop the appropriate use of historical terms. • Construct informed responses that involve thoughtful selection and organisation of relevant historical information.
Assess and review		• To assess the half-term's work.

Medium-term planning Summer 2: Early Islamic civilisation

National Curriculum objective

Children should be taught about:
• a non-European society that provides contrasts with British history – one study chosen from: early Islamic civilisation, including a study of Baghdad *circa* AD900; Mayan civilisation *circa* AD900; Benin (West Africa) *circa* AD900-1300

W	Outcomes	Historical concepts
1	• Can locate early Islamic civilisation on a timeline and a map of the world. • Can evaluate the role and significance of writing in the rise of early Islamic civilisation.	• Develop a chronologically secure knowledge and understanding of British, local and world history, establishing clear narratives within and across the periods they study. • Note connections, contrasts and trends over time. • Regularly address and sometimes devise historically valid questions about change, cause, similarity and difference, and significance.
2	• Can compare and contrast Islamic beliefs with Viking beliefs. • Can explain in simple terms the social structure of early Islamic civilisation.	• Develop a chronologically secure knowledge and understanding of British, local and world history, establishing clear narratives within and across the periods they study. • Regularly address and sometimes devise historically valid questions about change, cause, similarity and difference, and significance.
3	• Can explain the reasons why Baghdad was the centre of early Islamic civilisation. • Can compare and contrast daily life in Baghdad around AD900 with life in a Viking village at around the same time.	• Develop a chronologically secure knowledge and understanding of British, local and world history, establishing clear narratives within and across the periods they study. • Regularly address and sometimes devise historically valid questions about change, cause, similarity and difference, and significance.
4	• Can explain the significance of Baghdad's House of Wisdom. • Can describe some of the contributions to mathematics made by early Islamic scholars.	• Develop a chronologically secure knowledge and understanding of British, local and world history, establishing clear narratives within and across the periods they study. • Note connections, contrasts and trends over time. • Regularly address and sometimes devise historically valid questions about change, cause, similarity and difference, and significance.
5	• Can describe some of the contributions to science made by early Islamic scholars. • Can describe some forms of Islamic art, in terms of both media and motifs.	• Develop a chronologically secure knowledge and understanding of British, local and world history, establishing clear narratives within and across the periods they study. • Regularly address and sometimes devise historically valid questions about change, cause, similarity and difference, and significance.
6	• Can describe early Islamic architecture. • Can devise historically valid questions about early Islamic civilisation. • Can research answers to their questions, evaluating the sources they use for reliability.	• Develop a chronologically secure knowledge and understanding of British, local and world history, establishing clear narratives within and across the periods they study. • Regularly address and sometimes devise historically valid questions about change, cause, similarity and difference, and significance. • Construct informed responses that involve thoughtful selection and organisation of relevant historical information. • Understand how our knowledge of the past is constructed from a range of sources.
Assess and review		• To assess the half-term's work.

Year 6 Background knowledge

The Year 6 content begins by continuing the chronological narrative of British history. Children consolidate their knowledge of the Anglo-Saxons, developed in Year 5, by considering the impact of the first Viking raids along the British coast, and of the subsequent invasion and settlement of parts of Britain by Vikings. The chapters in the spring term extend children's knowledge of an aspect of British social history (medicine) beyond ancient times, into the Middle Ages and the modern era. The first chapter in the summer term continues in a similar vein, with a look at a significant turning point in British history: the Battle of Britain. The final chapter in Year 6 looks at early Islamic civilisation and draws comparisons with Viking society. While topics follow the chronological history of Britain and the wider world, core history skills should develop as children progress through the different topics and have been woven into the content planning.

Understanding chronology and timelines

In Year 6, children develop their understanding of chronology, considering events and civilisations that existed in different areas of the world within the same time period (Vikings in Britain running alongside the rise of early Islamic civilisation). They build on their understanding from Year 5 of how different historical periods fit together (the first Viking raids in AD793 to the death of Edward the Confessor in 1066). Children are given many opportunities to progress their skills in interpreting and constructing timelines to show when significant events occurred. They understand that these can cover short-term timescales (King Alfred's defence of his kingdom against the Vikings) or long-term timescales of over a thousand years (changes in medicine from Anglo-Saxon times to the present day).

Addressing and devising historically valid questions

In every topic, children have many opportunities to address historically valid questions (should Ethelred have paid the Danegeld? Why did the bubonic plague kill so many people? How did Edwin Chadwick advance medical knowledge? What was the strategy behind the Blitz?) using a range of reliable sources to find answers. Particularly when using the internet, it is important that children understand the difference between a reliable and non-reliable source of information and between fact and opinion. At the end of chapters 4 and 6, children are given the opportunity to devise their own historically valid questions and to carry out an independent investigation into an area of personal interest on the topics of medicine and early Islamic civilisation, sharing their findings through a project or presentation.

Constructing and interpreting the past from evidence

As children progress as historians, they view the past less in terms of facts and more as knowledge constructed from evidence. This evidence could be written (newspaper accounts from the Battle of Britain), from archaeological sites (digs in the Viking Age strata of York) or artefacts (early Islamic pottery), or even from eyewitness reports (interviews with elderly people recalling the polio outbreak of the 1940s and 1950s). In Year 6, children also progress in their understanding that evidence of the past is interpreted in different ways and that historical people and events can be viewed differently. Children begin to use the evidence to construct their own interpretations.

Understanding cause, consequence and significance

In the different topics, children have opportunities to consider the cause and consequences of different events (such as the events leading up to the Battle of Britain, and its immediate and longer-term consequences). Children examine the reasons behind events as well as the events themselves. This gives a good starting point for understanding which events can be considered historically significant (the discovery of penicillin).

Drawing comparisons

Throughout the scheme of work, there are opportunities for children to make observations and draw comparisons. In Year 6, they consider the similarities and differences between past civilisations (Viking burial compared with ancient Maya burial) as well as comparing life in the past with life today (the first hospitals compared with modern day hospitals).

Analysing change and trends over time

In Year 6, children develop the ability to analyse historical change and spot trends over time. As their knowledge base grows and they add to the knowledge they acquired in Year 5, certain historical themes and patterns emerge (social structure and slavery; invasion, oppression and assimilation of the existing population; the impact of technology).

Progression across the key stages

Progression in chronological understanding

Key Stage 1

Year 1	Year 2
• To know where people and events they study fit within a chronological framework. (NC)	• To know where people and events they study fit within a chronological framework. (NC) • To develop an awareness of the past, using common words and phrases relating to the passing of time. (NC)

Key Stage 2

Year 3	Year 4	Year 5	Year 6
• To develop a chronologically secure knowledge and understanding of British, local and world history. (NC) • To show awareness that the past can be divided into different historical periods.	• To develop a chronologically secure knowledge and understanding of British, local and world history. (NC) • To increasingly recognise that the past can be divided into different period of time.	• To continue to develop a chronologically secure knowledge and understanding of British, local and world history. (NC) • To make appropriate use of dates and terms.	• To continue to develop a chronologically secure knowledge and understanding of British, local and world history. (NC) • To understand chronology, and sequence British, local and world history using appropriate terms related to the passing of time.

Progression in historical enquiry skills

Key Stage 1

Year 1	Year 2
• To ask and answer questions about the past by making simple observations from stories and other sources. • To begin to understand some of the ways in which we find out about the past and identify different ways in which it is represented. (NC)	• To ask and answer questions, choosing and using parts of stories and other sources to show that they know and understand features of events. (NC) • To understand some of the ways in which we find out about the past and identify different ways in which it is represented. (NC)

Key Stage 2

Year 3	Year 4	Year 5	Year 6
• To begin to understand how our knowledge of the past is constructed from a range of sources. (NC) • To suggest methods of finding answers by using historical sources.	• To understand how our knowledge of the past is constructed from a range of sources. (NC) • To find answers to questions about the past by using sources of information.	• To begin to construct informed responses that involve thoughtful selection and organisation of relevant historical information. (NC) • To begin to select and combine information about the past in order to find answers to historical questions and test hypotheses.	• To begin to construct informed responses that involve thoughtful selection and organisation of relevant historical information. (NC) • To select and combine information about the past in order to support an historical enquiry, test hypotheses and evaluate success.

Progression in historical knowledge and understanding

Key Stage 1

Year 1	Year 2
• To develop an awareness of the past. (NC) • To learn about changes within living memory. (NC) • To learn about the lives of significant individuals in the past. (NC) • To learn about significant historical events, people and places in own locality. (NC)	• To develop an awareness of the past. (NC) • To learn about events beyond living memory that are significant nationally or globally. (NC) • To learn about the lives of significant individuals in the past. (NC) • To learn about significant historical events, people and places in own locality. (NC)

Key Stage 2

Year 3	Year 4	Year 5	Year 6
• To begin to develop knowledge and understanding of British, local and world history. (NC) • To begin to give a few reasons for, and results of, the main events and changes.	• To develop secure knowledge and understanding of British, local and world history, establishing clear narratives within and across the periods they study. (NC) • To give reasons for and/or results of the main events and changes.	• To develop secure knowledge and understanding of British, local and world history, establishing clear narratives within and across the periods they study. (NC) • To note connections, contrasts and trends over time and develop the appropriate use of historical terms. (NC)	• To develop secure knowledge and understanding of British, local and world history, establishing clear narratives within and across the periods they study. (NC) • To note connections, contrasts and trends over time and develop the appropriate use of historical terms. (NC) • To use their knowledge and understanding to describe the characteristics features of past societies and periods.

Planning a local history study

Local history provides opportunities for cross-curricular, hands-on history that is accessible to all.

How to choose a local history study?

The topic must have a local dimension, but this can be fairly broad – from the choice of a wide geographical area to that of a particular building or historical monument.

The topic could focus on a single curriculum-linked period of British history or range over several periods, as appropriate.

Consider how the study will enable children to examine change over time

Investigate whether you can tie your locality to a particularly significant national event alternatively, is there something that happened locally that had national repercussions?

Apply the same principles as above to people. Is there a significant local individual who affected your locality or events nationally?

Other starting points to consider

The school: start from where you are! Check for old registers, school newsletters, parish magazines, local building records and so on. A school study would be a particularly useful pathway for studying change over time.

Shops: examine photos and records of your local high street over a set period of time. Examine the buildings themselves and the shopping practices now and 'then'.

Hospitals: trace the history of medical provision in your area. Start with a 'care' map of the area showing hospitals, doctors' surgeries and clinics.

Place names and street names: walk the streets. Study maps. Who or what are the streets named after? Invite children to tell the story of the events that gave names to streets or buildings (they often give valuable clues to a town's industrial past or the achievements of notable individuals.)

Sports clubs: pose some historical questions around the origins of your local football (or other sports) club. Does their name have significance? When were they formed and why? Secondary resources (for example, web site and books) might well be useful for this task.

Monuments and statues: anything from monuments to plaques on the side of buildings can be useful starting points for historical enquiry.

Historic buildings: anything from stately homes to town halls or market squares can offer valuable starting points for historical study. Castles and churches are of particular interest. This could lead to developing a historical town trail.

Transport links: coaching inns, bridges, canals, old railway lines, toll gates can all offer wonderful starting points.

Events: this could be anything from Guy Fawkes celebrations in Lewes, Sussex to the annual handing out of 'buns' at the almshouses in Bedworth, Warwickshire.

People: history is about the lives of human beings. Focusing upon an individual provides can open many doors to the past.

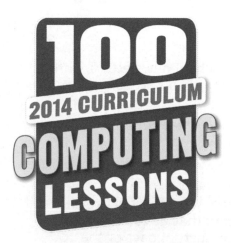
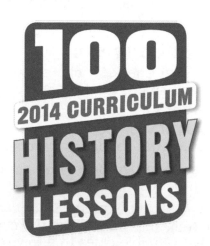
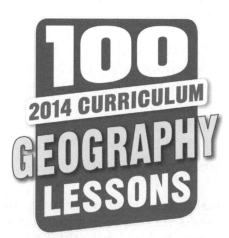